Edmund S. Ffoulkes

The Athanasian Creed

Edmund S. Ffoulkes

The Athanasian Creed

ISBN/EAN: 9783337318901

Printed in Europe, USA, Canada, Australia, Japan

Cover: Foto ©Lupo / pixelio.de

More available books at **www.hansebooks.com**

THE ATHANASIAN CREED:

BY WHOM WRITTEN

AND

BY WHOM PUBLISHED;

WITH OTHER

ENQUIRIES ON CREEDS IN GENERAL.

BY

THE REV. E. S. FFOULKES, B.D.

LATE FELLOW AND TUTOR OF JESUS COLLEGE, OXFORD;
AUTHOR OF "CHRISTENDOM'S DIVISIONS," ETC.

LONDON:
J. T. HAYES, LYALL PLACE, EATON SQUARE;
& 4, HENRIETTA STREET, COVENT GARDEN.

TO

BARTLE I. L. FRERE, ESQ.

IN GRATEFUL ACKNOWLEDGMENT

OF NEVER-TO-BE REPAID KINDNESS,

THIS WORK IS INSCRIBED,

BUT WITHOUT COMMITTING HIM TO ITS CONTENTS,

WITH THE BEST WISHES AND REGARDS

OF

THE AUTHOR

CONTENTS.

	PAGE
PREFACE	1

CHAPTER I.
THE EXPOSITION OF THE CREED BY RUFINUS . . . 11

II.
THE ROMAN CREED 81

III.
FROM CREEDS VARIABLE TO CREEDS FIXED AND UNIFORM 134

IV.
THE AGE, AIM, AND AUTHORSHIP OF THE ATHANASIAN CREED 189

V.
THE ATHANASIAN CREED A COMPILATION, NOT AN ORIGINAL WORK 278

VI.
CONCLUDING REMARKS 351

PREFACE.

THREE or four years ago I ventured to illustrate some general remarks on the rupture between the Latin and Greek Churches, by reference to the Athanasian Creed, as follows:—

"Whether from wilfulness, or from sheer ignorance, whether to give colour to their separation from the Greek Empire, or to gratify the passion for mythology, that even Christianity cannot eradicate from the heart of man, there can be no doubt but that one of the principal occupations of men of letters in the West, contemporary with Charlemagne, must have been to fabricate documents under fictitious names, and multiply pseudonymous compositions on every subject of public interest at that date. According to the absence or presence of malicious motives in the minds of those who framed them, legends or lies would be their proper name. But as the effect which they were designed to have was decidedly practical, so it has been far more pestiferous, we may be allowed to hope, than any of their most ardent votaries could have intended. There was an air of positiveness, assurance, and menace about them highly characteristic of the autocrat, and powerfully ministering to the naturally domineering propensities of the Latin mind, that stood out in marked contrast to the genuine freedom and philanthropy of the Gospel, and to the hitherto large and free spirit of the Church. To instance the most perfect specimen of the kind in all other respects, the Athanasian Creed: claiming at least equal antiquity with the Nicene, besides identity with it as regards doctrine. The

Nicene Fathers having set forth the faith of the Church in terms taken from Scripture, with one exception, end by anathematising the maintainers of certain errors, which are carefully specified: 'Those who say there was a time when the Son of God was not, or that He was not before He was begotten, or that He was begotten after the manner of a creature'—and so forth, but only those—only those are anathematised who had actually transgressed. How different the tenor of the Athanasian Creed, which, after setting forth the faith of the Church, reasoned out with extraordinary precision, but couched in anything but Scriptural language, finishes with the sweeping sentence: 'This is the Catholic faith, which, *except a man believe faithfully, he cannot be saved.*' While the Church in Council is content in denouncing a specific class of persons obstinately maintaining errors opposed to the leading articles of her public creed, a private doctor is made to pronounce the salvation of all impossible, who are not faithful believers in every single particular of his own dogmatic statement. Whether the Athanasian Creed itself set the fashion, or was drawn up to suit a fashion already set, the resemblance between it and the known formularies of the age of Charlemagne is, to say the least, very striking.

This is the Catholic faith,' says Charlemagne of the creed *paraphrased by himself*, ' which every one keeping whole and undefiled will have everlasting life.' And Leo III., in the profession attributed to him, but in any case submitted to Charlemagne before it was published: ' He that believes not according to this right faith is damned by the Catholic and Apostolic Church.' " *

In a former chapter, I had shown conclusively, that "*in point of fact*" the

---

* " Christendom's Divisions," Part II., c. x. pp. 553-4.

Athanasian Creed was first used for controversial purposes against the Greeks: and that the effect of it had been to set up a fictitious antiquity for Latin doctrine, analogous to what had been set up through the False Decretals for Latin discipline.* On its authorship, having only conjecture to put forward at that time, I forebore to speculate; but resolved to take the earliest opportunity that offered of coming to a sound conclusion. This has been commenced and laid aside again and again, on the plan of making an independent search: a task rendered infinitely less formidable than it used to be, by the judicious arrangements of the Reading Room in the British Museum, where the invaluable Patristic Series of Abbé Migne, comprising almost every line that has ever been printed of ecclesi-

---

* Chap. viii., pp. 429-30.

astical literature from the first to the middle of the thirteenth century, has been placed within easy access of every reader, so that it would be unpardonable for any such in future to be content to quote second-hand, instead of going to the originals for themselves. Had I read Waterland and other moderns on the Athanasian Creed at the beginning instead of at the end of my inquiry, I should have probably given up in despair a problem that had baffled so many wiser heads than my own: or from looking at its various surroundings through their spectacles, made no real progress beyond them in detecting its clue. Even now the number of accepted conclusions that I must challenge before my own is reached appals me. Still was it not in this way precisely that they came to theirs? When Voss published his celebrated treatise " On the Three Creeds," he was aghast at his own boldness in maintaining that the Athanasian Creed had not been written by S. Athanasius, or by a Greek at all; and that the Apostles' Creed could not have been possibly composed by the Apostles. Both statements fell upon Western Christendom like a thunder-clap; and were regarded as little short of sacrilege by the majority; few ventured to give them a hearing, still fewer to accept them publicly.* Now, there is not a learned man in any communion

---

* Comber testifies to the prevailing opinion, in spite of all that Ussher had written in support of Voss—"All which hath prevailed with the sober and learned men of these ages, whether Roman or Reformed, Lutheran or Calvinistical, to assent to his truth, as may be seen in the writings of many Roman doctors; and in the works of M. Luther, of Calvin, Beza, P. Martyr, and Bullinger; as also in the public Confessions and Articles of the Churches of England, Saxony, France, Bohemia, etc., this Creed is asserted to be the Apostles' own composition." — "Companion to the Temple," Part I., c. 17.

who would dispute them. In the Catechism of the Council of Trent, to be sure, which the Roman clergy must teach as gospel to this day, the old story that the Apostles, under inspiration of the Holy Ghost, arranged the creed called after them "in twelve articles," is told at length;* and in the rubrics of the English Prayer Book directions are given for the use of "the Apostles' Creed," and of the "Creed of S. Athanasius," as though both had been called by their right names; still all educated Roman Catholics, as well as Anglicans, have long been too well informed not to know that the supposed authorship of both has been utterly exploded; and that neither, in reality, was composed as its name would imply.

By whom they were composed, indeed,

---

* Part I., c. 1.

is a further problem which has not yet been solved; and it is just here that the labours of Voss and others require to be supplemented, or even revised. For they left standing, or rather they acquiesced in, several positions as untenable as those which they overthrew—among them these two particularly: 1. That the creed known to us as the Apostles' Creed was, in reality, that of the Roman Church; and 2. That the distinctive name which it now bears was given to it at a very early period. They had positively no ground for either position, but what was *supposed* to be contained in a well-known " Exposition " of this creed, *supposed* latterly to have been written by Rufinus, a presbyter of Aquileia, a town in north Italy, towards A.D. 400.

There are two suppositions here:

1. What Rufinus was supposed to have written; and

2. What was supposed to be contained in it.

I shall hope to throw some light upon both in my first chapter.

CHAPTER I.

ON THE EXPOSITION OF THE CREED BY RUFINUS.

RUFINUS TORANUS, or Tyrannius, as he was surnamed, is said to have been a native of Concordia, a town of North Italy, near Aquileia, then the capital of Istria, at the head of the Adriatic, on the northeast. And neither his personal character, nor his travels, ought to be quite passed over in any critical examination of his writings. The year of his birth is uncertain; but he was baptized at Aquileia, as he tells us in the fifth chapter of the first book of his "Apology," after having spent thirty years there in a monastery, and been instructed in the faith and creed previously to receiving baptism by a deacon of the church there, named Eusebius. A.D. 371 is generally supposed to have been the date of his baptism; and soon afterwards he started, in company with a Roman lady named Melania, who from that time seems to have been his travelling companion through life, for Egypt, where he spent six years, off and on, among the monks of Nitria. Then quitting Egypt for Palestine, he fixed his head-quarters for twenty years or more in a convent on Mount Olives, and so became intimate with John, Bishop of Jerusalem, by whom he was ordained presbyter, and with whom he sided against SS. Epiphanius and Jerome, in their hot controversy respecting the works of Origen, in which all shocked Christendom equally by their intemperate language, perhaps he most of all. A.D. 397, he re-visited Italy, and spent some time at Rome, adding fuel to the flame;

and being in the end severely reprimanded, if not excommunicated as a heretic, in consequence, by Pope Anastasius. This induced him to keep quiet at Aquileia for the next ten years, notwithstanding its siege by the Goths; and when, A.D. 411, he next set out on his travels, it was to die in Sicily. Rufinus so far profited by his travels as to become thoroughly conversant with the Greek language, which he might never have learnt so well at home; and his translations from Greek into Latin were most extensive, though exhibiting nothing of the conscientious exactness of his once friend and near neighbour, S. Jerome. Among them were the "Antiquities and Wars of the Jews," by Josephus; several of the works of Origen; several of the then *reputed* works of S. Clement of Rome; and the ten books of "Ecclesiastical History," by Eusebius, which he supplemented by two of his own. Of these last, Socrates, the historian, says that he had followed them implicitly, till he had discovered how many mistakes they contained.* And of his translations generally, Cave says with great truth: "It cannot be denied that Rufinus in translating the works of others, acted for the most part in bad faith, by changing, mutilating, and adding to that extent as to make them appear originals rather than composed by others, so that nobody can divine with certainty which parts are by him, and which by their real authors."†

Aquileia, the city to whose Church Rufinus was attached, had a history of its own likewise. It was situated, as has been said, at the head of the Adriatic, about a dozen miles from the sea, with which it communicated by rivers, and in becoming a Roman colony, B.C. 180, was designed to be the bulwark of Italy against the barbarous tribes of Illyria and Pannonia to the north-east. Strongly fortified against these, but with increased

* Hist. II. 1. † Hist. Lit. I. v.

security, therefore, for commerce, it attained such eminence in a short time that it ranked only second to Rome;* and of course when Illyria and Pannonia became Roman provinces, it became their emporium as well; the frontier town, through which all the luxuries and world-wide produce filtered from the seat of empire to the new territory, and to which all the aspiring but untutored spirits in the new territory flocked to be schooled in accomplishments. Aquileia was therefore both a commercial and a border town of the first order, seething with life, when it received Christianity; and being situated between the extremes of barbarism and civilisation, it must have been inhabited by a motley, though stirring, race; and spoke a language—" Canusini more bilinguis "—that was far from pure. This may account also for several peculiarities in the character of

* "Herodiano l. viii. c. 2, Roma, seu Romania dicta, quia florente Imperio secundum semper locum obtinuit" ... Hoffman I. v.

Rufinus, commented upon by Cave and others.

Again, the invasion of the Goths and Ostrogoths, their more permanent settlements in the Danubian provinces, and in Thrace and Italy, *coupled with their adoption of Arianism*, cannot have failed to tinge the theological mind of the Aquileian Church, any more than those border influences thus aggravated the general tone of the city. And this may help us to appreciate several ecclesiastical as well as theological developments that occurred there subsequently to his time. When Aquileia was sacked and destroyed by Attila, A.D. 452, the jurisdiction of its Metropolitan, extended over Istria and the whole of Venetia, comprising no less than twenty-seven suffragan Sees.* But after it had been restored partially by

---

* See Diss. III. "De Conc. Forojul." by Madrisius, editor of the works of S. Paulinus: (Patrol. xcix., 533-46) showing the extent of its jurisdiction at various times.

Narses, a new phenomenon—and one that has remained unique ever since—arose there, curiously symbolical of its character as a border-town: an Eastern dignity, that of patriarch, assumed by a Western prelate. Further, this distinction was assumed by him not merely without consulting Rome, but at the commencement of a long schism from Rome: which schism again was equally characteristic, as on the point which gave rise to it, the condemnation of the three chapters, as they were called, the heads of the Western and Eastern communions—Rome and Constantinople—were agreed. Such was also the tenacity with which the Aquileian church upheld its own acts, in spite of all the later reverses endured by the city, and even its own temporary removal to Grado, that its patriarchs were not merely recognised in their new dignity by Rome when the schism ceased, but, notwithstanding a fresh act of disloyalty committed by one of them in siding with

Photius, John XIX. was content to speak of the See of Aquileia, two centuries later, as being second in rank to Rome, and above all other Episcopal sees throughout Italy. In short, 150 years have barely elapsed since the Patriarch of Aquileia ceased to exist, though the See of Venice formally received a grant of his dignity from Nicholas V. three centuries earlier, or three years before Constantinople fell into the hands of the Turks.

Such was Aquileia, and such Rufinus, its presbyter, to whom, as author of a commentary upon the specific creed of the Aquileian church, almost all learned men have for the last three centuries appealed exclusively for the origin and true character of what is called the Apostles' Creed; and that he did actually write some such commentary, nay, some part of the commentary now bearing his name, cannot be denied, as we shall see. But this is altogether beside the real question. The question which I am about to propose to the learned, and hope to supply them with materials for deciding, is, Whether Rufinus has been more interpolated than misunderstood, or more misunderstood than interpolated.

I begin, then, by expressing my surprise that the learned should not have bestowed more criticism upon a work on which they have built so much. It used, indeed, to be difficult of access to students. It has recently been reprinted in a very convenient shape by Professor Heurtley, among the documents forming his smaller manual, entitled "De Fide et Symbolo," which, in fact, put it into my own hands portably for the first time. Tendering, therefore, my hearty acknowledgments to the Professor for the boon or its text, he must allow me, nevertheless, to regret that he should have told us so little about its history, and that he should not have made more use of his own proximity to the Bodleian and Christ Church libraries to verify what others had written of it before following them, as well as to inform us whether any different views had been current about it before or since. In his brief notice of Rufinus, he says it has been printed from the text of Vallarsius;* accordingly, when its turn comes, it appears headed "Commentarius in Symbolum Apostolorum, Tyrannio Rufino Aquileiensi Presbytero Auctore," † which is the title given to it by Vallarsius, but on what authority the Lady Margaret Professor forbears to ask; and I cannot discover that Vallarsius could have produced any. That the earliest discoverable should have‡ been the Oxford Edition of S. Cyprian, A.D. 1692, numerous as the editions of it had been for 200 years previously, ought, surely, to have been stated; and one would have supposed an Oxford editor might have felt interest in recording that it was *first* printed at Oxford, being one

* P. 29, † P. 101.
‡ Append. III., p. 17.

of the first books ever printed in England, as "Beati Hieronymi expositio in symbolo Apostolorum ad Papam Laurentium," A.D., 1468, from which title we should have learnt at once that in those days it was attributed not to Rufinus, but to S. Jerome. So it was printed at Oxford again, A.D. 1498; at Rome, A.D. 1470 and 1576, as "Expositio in Symbolum," with the letters of S. Jerome; at Basle, A.D. 1519, as "Symbolum fidei," with the works of S. Cyprian; at Paris, A.D. 1570, as "Commentarius in Symbolum," in a separate form.* Schœnnemann's title† for it, in giving it to Rufinus, is, "Explicatio symboli."

The truth is, and should have been stated therefore, that few treatises have ever been printed under so many different titles, or shifted about more to one author after another. How it came to be so long dissevered from Rufinus and his other

* See the list in Migne's Patrol. xxi. 17-20.
† Ibid. 15.

works is for those moderns who have concluded it to be his as it stands, not for me, to explain. But one MS. of any reputed antiquity connects it with his name; and even there "Incipit Expositio symboli sancti Rufini" reads like a clerical error for "Hieronymi," or some one else, for Rufinus is not known generally to literature as a saint. To return to the heading of Vallarsius, the probability is that he took it from the Oxford edition of S. Cyprian, A.D. 1682, and the Oxford editors, Bishops Fell and Pearson, from the first printed edition of this exposition— namely, that of Oxford, A.D. 1468, substituting, on their own authority, "Rufini" for "Hieronymi." But here they should have reflected that if one part of their adopted heading required correction, so might another; and a very brief inquiry would have convinced them that the word "Apostolorum" should have been ejected, intrinsic as well as extrinsic evidence being opposed to it. Neither S. John

Cassian nor Gennadius, on whose authority Rufinus has come to be credited with this Exposition—the former writing within fifty years of its supposed publication—speaks of his having commented on the "*Creed of the Apostles*," but merely the "Creed;" and Cassian, in fact, applies what Rufinus had said of the apostolic origin of the Creed in general (unless, indeed, this passage was afterwards introduced into his work from Cassian) to the Creed then current in the Church of Antioch, on which he is engaged himself. In the same way S. Augustine, writing about the same time, and commenting upon the same Creed practically with Rufinus, fixed the title of his own treatise by naming it in his Retractations "De Fide ac Symbolo." His sermons to Catechumens contain their own title—viz., "De Symbolo;" likewise, S. Maximus of Turin published homilies in the next generation, "De Traditione Symboli;" and S. Nicetas of Aquileia shortly afterwards explained the identical Creed on which Rufinus had written in a treatise still called " Explanatio symboli habita ad competentes." It is true that seven sermons of S. Peter Chrysologus of Ravenna, preached about the same time, are now headed " De Symbolo Apostolorum ;" but the last word is wholly unauthorised by anything they contain. Besides, that having been all preached on a special occasion, like the homilies of S. Maximus—viz., " The delivery of the Creed to the baptized"—they must have been designated originally from the phrase for it which was then in use. Now, this phrase was invariably " Traditio Symboli," without any further addition. Even the treatise by Venantius Fortunatus, supposed to have been written at the commencement of the seventh century, and founded on this of Rufinus, is entitled " Expositio Symboli." But, indeed, the text of this Exposition is of itself fatal to its modern title. It begins by discoursing on the Creed in general; then, after admonishing the reader that additional Articles were found in one Church's Creed that were not in another's,* it selects that of the Church of Aquileia for comment. As it proceeds, it notices various points on which this Creed differed from other forms current elsewhere, till at last we come to the following passage,† "As is also said in the Creed: ' Whose kingdom shall have no end ;'" which may be considered decisive of the question at issue—this Article being peculiar to the Eastern form of the Creed, at the same time that it is acknowledged by the author of this Exposition in express terms to be part of the Creed on which he was then commenting.

If it is Rufinus who is here speaking, he clearly could not have dreamt of ex-

---

* Illud non inopportune commonendum puto, quòd in diversis ecclesiis aliqua in his verbis inveniuntur adjecta. § 3.

† § 34.

pounding what we call the Apostles' Creed apart from the rest, or known it distinguished from all other existing forms by that name.

There is indeed another, and a much more celebrated statement in this treatise, which has given rise to the idea that he was; but as it is just one of those passages which determine this treatise not to be his in its existing form, I shall refrain from quoting it till its turn comes for that purpose.

What has made critics so ready to concur in attributing this treatise to him is simply this: First, it wanted an author, after it had been pronounced not to be the work of either S. Cyprian or S. Jerome; secondly, it professed to have been written by a member of the Church of Aquileia; thirdly, Rufinus, one of the best known members of that church, is pointedly stated by Cassian and Gennadius to have written a treatise of this kind—pointedly stated, as there is considerable point of one kind or another in both passages.

Gennadius wrote latest, so let us commence with him. In the printed editions of his "Catalogue of Illustrious Men," he speaks as follows, amongst other things, of Rufinus: "By his own diligence, or rather by the gift of the grace of God, the same Rufinus so expounded the Creed, *that others may be deemed, in comparison of him, not to have expounded it at all.*" But in a very old, if not the oldest MS. of this work of Gennadius, the words following "expounded the Creed" are not found; the words preceding "Rufinus" indeed are no longer legible, still there is space left which they *may* have once filled. But there is no space for the laudatory sentence coming after the word "Creed" in the printed editions.[*] If Rufinus has been interpolated, Gennadius also may have been interpolated by his interpolator, to add

[*] I give the MS. and the printed version as they

lustre to his own performance. What says John Cassian?*

"Rufinus also testifies, in his "*Exposition of the Creed*," as follows, on our Lord's Incarnation: "The Son of God," he says, "was born of a Virgin, not being united to the flesh only, nor principally; but having a soul intermediate between the flesh and God."

These words occurring in the thirteenth section of this Exposition, we may not doubt some parts of it having been penned by Rufinus. But even Cassian suggests doubts of the whole being his in its present

stand in the Ben. Edit. of S. Jerome, vol. v. p. 49 and *seq.*

Codex MS.	*Editi Libri.*
Rufinus symbolum disseruit, et Benedictiones Jacob supra Patriarchas .... mystico sermone.	Exposuit idem Rufinus symbolum, ut in ejus comparatione alii non exposuisse videantur. Disseruit et benedictionem Jacob super Patriarchas .... mystico sensu.

Cave says of this work: "Extat longè integrior in Cod. MS. Corb:" which is this. Hist. Lit. iii. 5.

* De Incarn. vii. 27.

shape; for in another chapter,* while repeating and appropriating, as I have said before, the explanation, if genuine, which is there given of the word "symbolum," he omits all reference to the traditional story by which this is prefaced: the "*locus classicus*" in later ages, and from then till now, of the whole work: and which, literally translated, runs thus:—

"*Tradunt majores*,† our ancestors relate, that after our Lord's Ascension,

---

* I put them in parallel columns:

Cassian.

Symbolum, ut scis, ex collatione nomen accepit. Quod enim Græcè σύμβολον dicitur, Latinè collatio nominatur. Collatio autem ideò, quia in unum collatâ ab Apostolis Domini totius Catholicæ legis fide, quidquid per universum divinorum voluminum corpus immensâ funditur copiâ, totum in symboli colligitur brevitate perfectâ, secundum illud Apostoli; "verbum," inquit, "consummans et brevians in æquitate; quia verbum breviatum faciet Dominus super terram"—Hist.Lit. vi. 3.

Rufinus.

Symbolum autem hoc multis at justissimis ex causis appellari voluerunt. Symbolum enim Græcè et indicium dici potest et collatio, hoc est, quod plures in unum conferunt. Id enim fecerunt Apostoli in his sermonibus, in unum conferendo unusquisque quod sensit. . . . . § 2.

In his verè comperitur prophetia quæ dicit: "Verbum enim consummans, et brevians in æquitate; quia verbum breviatum faciet Dominus super terram"—§ 1.

† § 2.

when by the coming of the Holy Ghost fiery tongues had sat upon each of the Apostles, so that they spake with diverse tongues, causing no nation to seem foreign to them, nor any barbarisms of language impervious or inaccessible, they received commandment of the Lord to go and preach His Word to all nations. Accordingly, being about to depart from each other, they first appointed themselves a rule mutually for their future preaching, lest, separated in different directions, any of them perchance should expound any thing differently to those whom they invited to the faith of Christ. All, therefore, being assembled in one place, and filled with the Holy Ghost, they compiled, as we have said, this brief token for themselves of their future preaching, by throwing together what each thought himself, and ordained that all believers should have this rule given them."* And more to the same effect further on.

* § 2.

This passage, in spite of Cassian writing as though he had never seen it, has for centuries been thought to imply that a definite creed of twelve articles was actually composed by the twelve Apostles before separating, each Apostle contributing one; and that it is on this identical Creed, enlarged only by the additions made to it in the Church of Aquileia, that Rufinus wrote. The first of these inferences I am not concerned to dispute; the author of this passage may or may not have *meant* to assert as much, or more probably did; all that I am concerned to show is that he and Rufinus were different persons in any case: that Rufinus, for several reasons, could not have written this passage at all, and that it is unquestionably but one of many that have since been added to his work. When I read it, in its present shape, for the first time, my impression was that it was all patchwork: I now hope to be able to prove this of some parts of it conclusively.

"*Tradunt majores,*" but who were they? Bingham[*] has given a list of the authorities usually cited, and I believe that it could not be enlarged materially; but of these SS. Isidore, Cassian, Maximus of Turin, and Leo, could not have been called "ancestors" by Rufinus, as they lived after him; nor again SS. Augustine, Jerome, and Ambrose, who were his contemporaries; what Tertullian, Origen, and S. Irenæus say is only general: to the effect that a rule of faith instituted by Christ had been taught by the Apostles, and handed down in the Church. There was one Father to be sure that was once thought to have spoken more definitely, S. Clement of Rome; and had he written really what was attributed to him, there might have been some ground for inferring that those who followed him could mean no less. But the letter in which this passage occurs has long since been proved spurious, and is always printed in

[*] Antiq. x. 3, 5.

its existing shape with the False Decretals. Let us understand, however, that it was *not all forged at the same time*, and that part of it, *most singularly*, had been in circulation a long time when Rufinus lived, and was actually one of the works translated by him from Greek into Latin. But this part ends abruptly with what is now the first half of chapter twenty; and it is in the twenty-first chapter, just where the pseudo-Isidorian addition begins, that the history of the formation of the Creed is epitomised, word for word, from this Exposition. The supposed letter of S. Clement, in its original shape, has been printed by Coteler,* with the Latin version of it by Rufinus immediately following; and in its enlarged shape by Hinschius among the pseudo-Decretals.† Anybody, then, who will be at the pains of examining both will see, that what used to be quoted as the chief authority for this

---

* Pat. Apost. i. 616.
† Tauchnitz edit. p. 37.

legendary tale which Rufinus is supposed to have penned, was actually not in existence when the letter, to which a summary of it has since been appended, was translated by Rufinus himself.

This coincidence would alone suffice to suggest grave doubt of the authorship of this Exposition as it stands now. What shook my faith in its authenticity first on reading it was its dedication. It is dedicated to a "most faithful Pope Laurence," whom nobody has ever been able to verify, save that by "pope" must be meant "bishop," or rather a bishop to whom more than ordinary deference was intended.* Now, it is not a little curious

---

* Bingham's own instances should have told him this (the italics are mine): "Dionysius, Presbyter of Alexandria, speaking of Heraclas, *his* bishop, gives him the very same title: 'the blessed pope' Heraclas. And Arius himself . . . speaks of *his* Bishop, Alexander, in the same style. S. Jerome gives the title to Athanasius, Epiphanius, and Paulinus; and writing often to S. Austin he *always* inscribes his epistles 'beatissimo papæ Augustino.'" . . I. ii. 7. Just so; but then he is

that a work so well known and esteemed as the "Euchiridion," or Manual "on Faith, Hope, and Charity," by S. Augustine, should have been also dedicated to a Laurence, but of whose identity S. Augustine informs us himself; and that, in consequence, part of the title given to it often in manuscripts has been, "Ad Laurentium primicerium notariorum urbis Romæ;" or, "Ad Laurentium diaconum," and so forth. A person emulous of the fame of this work might have aped its dedication in publishing a kindred performance of his own; nor possibly would Rufinus have been above doing this himself, had S. Augustine written *first*. But

far from calling *every* bishop "pope." All these are cases of presbyters addressing or speaking of bishops. S. Austin, on the other hand, is as particular in styling his Metropolitan Aurelius "pope," as in not giving any mere brother-bishop that style. Curiously enough, this is not the style employed by Rufinus himself in dedicating his Ecclesiastical History to Chromatius, Bishop of Aquileia, or his "Recognitions of S. Clement" to Gaudentius, Bishop of Brescia.

as Rufinus died A.D. 410, and S. Augustine speaks in his own treatise* of S. Jerome as dead likewise, his own cannot for certain have been given to the world till after the death of S. Jerome, which occurred A.D. 420. This suggested to me the possibility that the dedication of the work of Rufinus was fictitious, and a later addition. I have become convinced of it since, but upon different grounds.

Another doubt was suggested to me by what is said in various parts of this Exposition on the " descent into hell." " Rufinus himself," says Bingham,† " tells us, 'the descent into hell' was neither in the Roman Creed, which is that we call the Apostles' Creed, nor yet in any creed of the Eastern Churches: only the sense of it might be said to be couched in that other expression, ' He was buried.' " Bingham is quite correct so far, that this is the interpretation given to those words

* C. 87. † X. 315.

in one place, viz., § 18;* but he should have read on. They are explained very differently § 28, and again § 30; and in § 48, where the sum of all that had gone before purports to be resumed, the advantage of our Lord's descent into hell is stated to be the "recal of souls from captivity there," which is another thing altogether. This led me to inquire whether Rufinus had ever mentioned this article in connection with the Creed elsewhere. For, as most people know, who know anything at all of his history, he had at one time to defend himself against S. Jerome, and to clear himself to the Pope. And in each case he has left us a full account of his faith. Now, on both occasions, the heads of his faith, he maintains with emphasis, are taken from the Creed of the Church in which he had received catechetical instruction and been baptized; viz., the

* "Vis tamen verbi eadem videtur esse in eo quod 'sepultus' dicitur."

Church of Aquileia; but among these, "the descent into hell" is on neither occasion reckoned as one; nor is there the faintest allusion to it in either of any sort.* Again, the first article of the same Creed is in this Exposition stated expressly to have been: "I believe in God the Father Almighty, invisible and impassible;" these last two words, we are told, "having been added to it in consequence of the heresy of Sabellius, known

---

* Take what he says to the Pope, for instance: "Filium quoque Dei in novissimis diebus natum esse confitemur ex Virgine et Spiritu Sancto carnem naturæ humanæ atque animam suscepisse, in quâ passus est, et sepultus, et resurrexit a mortuis." . . . And then adds: "Hanc fidem—quam supra exposui—id est, quam ecclesia Romana, et Alexandrina, et Aquileiensis nostra tenet, quæque Hierosolymis prædicatur." See the Ben. Edit. of S. Jerome, vol. v. p. 259, where are printed also the "Damasi Symbolum," and "Symb. explan. ad Damasum," and "Expl. fidei ad S. Cyril," all composed about the same time, and equally silent on the "Descent into hell." So, too, is the treatise "De fide," given to Rufinus by Sirmond., Op. i. 160.

to our people"—by the Aquileians, that is
—" as the Patripassian;" the twofold inference from which would be, that the Aquileians were peculiar in designating Sabellius and his followers Patripassians, and that the Church of Aquileia had in time past been infested by this heresy to a much greater degree than its neighbours. The former is contrary to fact; the latter unsupported by anything that we read elsewhere. Rufinus, again, says nothing about this addition in vindicating his orthodoxy to S. Jerome and the Pope. Considering he was accused of Origenism, and defended himself, as has been said, by reference to the Creed of his Church —a Creed to which S. Jerome, a native of Dalmatia, could have been no stranger —this omission seemed as difficult to account for as the other. And both infinitely more so by contrast. For there is yet a third peculiarity declared in this Exposition to attach to the Creed of Aquileia; which not content with affirm-

ing "the resurrection of the body" as it stands in other Creeds, by adding the demonstrative pronoun, and changing it into "the resurrection of *this* body," seemed intent upon bringing it home to the individual each time that he professed his faith—"this body," namely, "with which I am now clothed." Now, in the fifth chapter of the first book of his work against S. Jerome, Rufinus attributes this peculiarity to the Aquileian Creed, and then expatiates upon it in terms so similar, that we can only conclude what he says there to have been copied from this Exposition, or this Exposition from what he says there. Thus of the three peculiarities attributed to the Aquileian Creed in this Exposition, Rufinus writing in his own person, and treating of the same subject, remarkably confirms the last, but altogether ignores the others.

Let us at once pass on to another work of the same kind, recently proved to have been written by a member of the Church of Aquileia, and in the same century, though somewhat later, with which this Exposition has not as yet been sufficiently compared—I mean the " Explanation of the Creed,"* addressed to candidates for baptism, by S. Nicetas, who became Bishop of Aquileia some fifty years after the death of Rufinus, and corresponded with Pope Leo I. Possibly the sack and destruction of Aquileia by the Huns, A.D. 452, may be one reason why the precise limits of his episcopate have proved so difficult to fix. Nobody could doubt on reading both works, that either S. Nicetas must have borrowed from this Exposition, or the author of this Exposition from Nicetas; and anybody that was unacquainted with their respective histories, would see cause to conclude that S. Nicetas wrote first; the simple truth being that he wrote before this work of Rufinus had

* In Migne's Patrol. lii. 865 *et seq.*, with P. Braida's Dissert.

been interpolated.* Braida,† the learned editor of S. Nicetas, from not having perceived this, is hopelessly bewildered to reconcile the accounts given by a presbyter and bishop of the same Church, separated only by fifty years from each other, of the Creed in use there; and hazards a conjecture, refuted beforehand, as we shall see, by what actually took place. S. Nicetas had his eyes on this Exposition, not as it stands now, but as it was originally penned by Rufinus, in writing his own. Like Rufinus in his work against S. Jerome, and in the genuine portion of this Exposition, he

* I instance the following as looking that way:

§ 18.	S. Nicetas.
Cautissimè autem qui symbolum tradiderunt etiam tempus quo hæc sub Pontio Pilato gesta sunt *designarunt*, ne ex aliquâ parte velut vaga et incerta gestorum traditio vacillaret.	Tempus *designatur*, quo Pontius Pilatus fuit præses Syriæ et Palestinæ. Hoc autem *cautè* ponitur, quia aliquanti hæreticorum demoniacis fraudibus decepti, diversos garriunt Christos.

Superlatives are rarely dwarfed into positives by copiers. This I take, therefore, to be another case of interpolation.

† M. Migne's Patrol. lii. p. 63, *et seq.*

lays stress upon the pronoun which in the Creed of Aquileia brought out the doctrine of the resurrection of the body with such marked emphasis: "It is in 'the resurrection of *your* body' that you profess belief," he tells his hearers. Like Rufinus writing in his own name, he notices no other peculiarity than this in the Creed explained by him, viz., that of his Church. What he says of its Apostolic origin is still more noteworthy: " This rule of faith the Apostles received from our Lord, that they should " baptize all nations in the name of the Father, and of the Son, and of the Holy Ghost:" thus tracing it back to the baptismal form, its undoubted, and therefore so far Apostolic, source. Contrast this explanation, so thoroughly real and intelligible with the legendary tale fathered upon Rufinus. The true Rufinus lives in this work of an Aquileian prelate, who may have been a child when he died; the false Rufinus, unrecognised in this work, is in harmony with the pseudo-Decretals published four hundred years after his death. Cassian's reticence, then, on which I remarked previously, can create no further surprise.

Let us now go back "to the descent into hell," which, in deference to this Exposition, has been supposed so generally to have formed part of the Aquileian Creed in the days of Rufinus, remembering always that the question is not whether any opinions had been expressed on this head by any of the Fathers as yet in commenting upon Scripture; but whether it was in the habit of being handled by them then in their discourses to catechumens, or insisted upon in expounding the Creed of the Church.

First, then, let it be said that this article was originally brought out in a semi-Arian Creed, that it was promulgated no less than four times by semi-Arian synods contemporary with Rufinus; and that, putting this Exposition on one side, there is no proof of its having formed part of any orthodox Creed before the seventh century. The heterodox Creed in which it appeared first, is now known as the third Sirmian, A.D. 357. This was accepted at Rimini, A.D. 359.* It was contained in that of the Synod of Nice in Thrace the same year;† and in that of Constantinople, A.D. 360.‡ If it was in the Aquileian Creed therefore, when Rufinus wrote, it must have been adopted from the semi-Arian creeds into this, or from this into them. We are not told even by the supposed Rufinus, who put it into the Aquileian Creed; we *know* that they were semi-Arians, who put it into those creeds of Sirmium, Rimini,

---

* Soc. ii. 37. † Theodor. ii. 21.

‡ Soc. ii. 41. They may be seen at length in Prof. Heurtley's "Harmonia Symbolica," but he draws no conclusion from them. As Pearson remarks, (on the Creed, vol. ii. 199, Oxford Edit.) "At Sirmium the *descent* was mentioned, and the *burial* omitted;" at Nice and Constantinople, "both the burial and the descent were mentioned."

Nice, and Constantinople. This circumstance may serve to explain several anomalies connected with its adoption as a dogma. The first person to whom it is ever stated to have been preached was Abgarus, King of Edessa, the preacher being either the Apostle, or one of the seventy disciples, named Thaddeus. Eusebius, the historian, whose semi-Arian connections are well known, avers he procured and translated the document containing this apocryphal tale himself from the Syrian archives.* Not many years after his death, S. Cyril, then a presbyter, delivered his catechetical lectures A.D. 348, at Jerusalem on the Creed, in which, though the Creed of Jerusalem contained no such article,† he asserts that "our Lord descended into the parts beneath the earth to liberate the just from thence." ‡ Two years afterwards he was consecrated

* E. H. i. 13.
† In Heurtley : " De fide," etc., p. 9.
‡ Ib. 47.

Bishop of Jerusalem by Acacius,* who had succeeded Eusebius, the historian, at Cæsarea: " had been his pupil, and on his death inherited his library;" and who was then the most distinguished for 'ability, learning, and unscrupulousness,' of the semi-Arian party.† S. Cyril, however, was not long in withdrawing from this connection on becoming bishop; and as he was deposed at the fourth of the semi-Arian Synods above-named,‡ in whose Creed the descent into hell was expressed, he would have been the last person, probably, to have advocated its insertion into the orthodox Creed just then. On the other hand, its adoption by the semi-Arians aided the orthodox materially just then, in refuting a new error usually charged upon Apollinarius, but, in reality, broached by them,§ to the effect that our Lord had

* Soc. ii. 38.
† Newman's "Arians," c. iv. § 1.
‡ Soc. ii. 42.
§ "Apollinaristas Apollinaris instituit, qui de animà Christi a Catholicis dissenserunt, dicentes,

only taken upon Him our flesh, and that His Divinity stood to Him in the place of a soul. For these heretics having made public profession of His descent into hell, the orthodox turned their position upon them at once, by rejoining that there was but one way of explaining it intelligibly, viz., that His soul had gone thither.* There are two distinct references to this error of theirs in what I take to be the genuine part of this Exposition, one of which is the passage cited in disproof of it by S. John Cassian;† but there is no reference whatsoever to its refutation by

sicut Ariani, Deum Christum carnem sine animâ suscepisse." S. Aug. de Hær. 55. The fragment from Eudoxius quoted by Gieseler, E. H. § 83, note 29, proves what S. Augustine says of the Arians.

* Pearson on the Creed, vol. ii. 203-5.

† Above, p. 28. The other is § 39. "Quod olim congregavit pertinax et prava contentio, asserens Christum carnem quidem humanam suscepisse, non tamen et animam rationalem." Apollinarius is not named: possibly because Eunomius, who held this also, was the last person spoken of.

means of our Lord's descent into hell in a single passage where that subject is handled. Would a topic like this have been unnoticed by Rufinus, had "the descent into hell" entered the orthodox Creed of his Church then? Four heterodox synods in succession had authorised it as we have seen during his lifetime: the first of them held at Sirmium, not far from where he lived, and it had been turned against them triumphantly by the orthodox. S. Nicetas in explaining the Creed of Aquileia within fifty years of his death, article by article, fails to testify to its existence there. S. Augustine commented on the Creed in Africa, S. Maximus at Turin, S. Peter Chrysologus at Ravenna, during the same period, without alluding to it. The only mention of it, in short, that I can find in any contemporary work designed for popular instruction, is in a sermon of S. Gaudentius, Bishop of Brescia, who was on intimate terms with Rufinus; and there it is explained in terms so similar to what occur in this Exposition,* that I am led to infer, not that what occur there were composed, or even inserted there, by Rufinus himself, but that they were *dove-tailed afterwards* into his work by his interpolator, from this discourse of his friend. It was to S. Gaudentius, strangely enough, that Rufinus dedicated his translation of the so-called "Recognitions of S. Clement," with the spurious letter of S. Clement already mentioned appended to them;

---

* *E.g.:*

§ 28.

Sed etiam quod in infernum descendit, *evidenter pronunciatur in Psalmis* . . . unde et Petrus dicit.

S. Gaud. Serm. viii.

De Exodi Lect.

Descendisse autem Salvatoris anima ad inferos visitandos, *non solum beati Petri epistola, verum etiam Davidis prophetia testatur.*

Again:

§ 48.

Quæ *utilitas divini ad inferna descensûs* . . . et *animarum* de infernis *revocata* captivitas.

S. Gaud. *Ibid.*

Filius enim Dei non *idcirco* cum suscepti hominis animâ *ad inferos descendit*, ut eam in inferno relinqueret, sed ut plurimas resurrecturis sanctorum corporibus *animas revocaret.*

and S. Gaudentius be it observed, is far from hinting in any of his sermons that the "descent into hell" formed part of his own, or any other Creed then. The profession of the Fourth Council of Toledo, A.D. 633, is the first orthodox profession extant and authentic that contains it. Once more, the substance of the account here given of those words " invisible and impassible" may be seen embodied in another well-known Arian profession, earlier by twelve years than the third Sirmian, and called from its unusual prolixity the Macrostyche;* which I shall cite further on.

Such are the grounds for concluding the possibility that this Exposition could have been written in its present shape by Rufinus to be small indeed; and such the principal interpolations occurring in it, to which I could add more, but none more

---

* Soc. ii. 19 (p. 100, 5; and 101, 15 *et seq*). Comp. S. Aug. Ep. 238 (al. 174), to Count Pascentius the Arian.

to the point.* If we now ask who interpolated it, we enter upon a much more difficult problem of course, and I can only suggest what may seem not improbable. In the twenty-third chapter of the second book of his work on "Ecclesiastical Offices,"† S. Isidore of Seville recites the legendary tale beginning with "*Tradunt majores,*" nearly word for word as

---

* This would be the list of them: First, the Dedication to "auditum," in § 1. Then from "Sed ut manifestius fiat," ... to "regulam statuunt," in § 2; and from "Discessuri igitur" to the end of that section. Then, from "His additur," in § 5, to the end of that section. The clause "Descendit in inferna," in § 14; and from "Cautissimò autem" ... to "dicitur," § 18, comprising the first explanation given of it; "Sed etiam quòd in infernum descendit"... to "descendentibus in locum, § 28; and, "Plenæ sunt his sacramentis," ... § 29, to "plura coacervare non possumus," at the end of § 30, comprising its second explanation. Lastly, "Sicut enim unus dicitur Pater," ... to "cuncta sanctificans," § 35 ; with the two clauses, "Quæ utilitas divini ad inferna descensus," ... et animarum de infernis revocata captivitas," § 48.

† There is a bit of it also quoted in his "Etym." vi. 19, 57.

it is now found, to nearly the end of the second chapter of this Exposition. This, if it existed there in his time, was of course the obvious thing for him to do, in treating of the Creed, yet tends to make the absence of any reference to it by SS. John Cassian and Nicetas all the more remarkable, had it existed there when they wrote. Again, S. Isidore, though he is the first writer who quotes it in full, is not the first writer who quotes it at all; to explain which properly we must turn over the records of his age with some care. Venantius Fortunatus, by some years his senior, according to Father Lucchi, was a native of Italy, pursued his studies at Ravenna, removed to a convent at Aquileia, was called Fortunatus from a saint much venerated at Aquileia of that name, passed into France just before the invasion of those parts by the Lombards, A.D. 568, became Bishop of Poitiers, A.D. 599, four years after the death of S. Gregory of Tours, with whom he was

to the point.* If we now ask who interpolated it, we enter upon a much more difficult problem of course, and I can only suggest what may seem not improbable. In the twenty-third chapter of the second book of his work on "Ecclesiastical Offices,"† S. Isidore of Seville recites the legendary tale beginning with "*Tradunt majores*," nearly word for word as

* This would be the list of them: First, the Dedication to "auditum," in § 1. Then from "Sed ut manifestius fiat," ... to "regulam statuunt," in § 2; and from "Discessuri igitur" to the end of that section. Then, from "His additur," in § 5, to the end of that section. The clause "Descendit in inferna," in § 14; and from "Cautissimè autem" ... to "dicitur," § 18, comprising the first explanation given of it; "Sed etiam quòd in infernum descendit" ... to "descendentibus in locum, § 28; and, "Plenæ sunt his sacramentis," ... § 29, to "plura coacervare non possumus," at the end of § 30, comprising its second explanation. Lastly, "Sicut enim unus dicitur Pater," ... to "cuncta sanctificans," § 35; with the two clauses, "Quæ utilitas divini ad inferna descensus," ... et animarum de infernis revocata captivitas," § 48.

† There is a bit of it also quoted in his "Etym." vi. 19, 57.

it is now found, to nearly the end of the second chapter of this Exposition. This, if it existed there in his time, was of course the obvious thing for him to do, in treating of the Creed, yet tends to make the absence of any reference to it by SS. John Cassian and Nicetas all the more remarkable, had it existed there when they wrote. Again, S. Isidore, though he is the first writer who quotes it in full, is not the first writer who quotes it at all; to explain which properly we must turn over the records of his age with some care. Venantius Fortunatus, by some years his senior, according to Father Lucchi, was a native of Italy, pursued his studies at Ravenna, removed to a convent at Aquileia, was called Fortunatus from a saint much venerated at Aquileia of that name, passed into France just before the invasion of those parts by the Lombards, A.D. 568, became Bishop of Poitiers, A.D. 599, four years after the death of S. Gregory of Tours, with whom he was intimate, and died in the first decade of the seventh century.* The eleventh book of his Miscellanies, which are in prose and verse, begins with an "Exposition of the Creed" in prose, supposed to have been written by him when bishop. "He who will compare this Exposition," says Lucchi, "with the one published among the works of Rufinus, cannot fail to perceive that the former is a mere epitome of the latter, and due to Rufinus rather than Fortunatus.† Father Lucchi was not aware of the existence of a similar treatise by S. Nicetas, equally revered at Aquileia with Rufinus; and as it had never occurred to him to question the genuineness of any part of the work of the latter, it never occurred to him, either,

* Vit. § 1-18, and then 26 and 89, in Migne's Patrol. lxxxviii. 23.

† Ad l. Braida on Nicet. p. 68, says the same. Prof. Heurtley, Harm. Symb. p. 55, is more guarded. "Venantius was evidently familiar with R.'s Exposition, of which he has frequently availed himself."

that Fortunatus was just as capable of expanding as of epitomising Rufinus, and of being served in each way himself subsequently by others. Father Lucchi would hardly seem to have scrutinised this work of his author with the care that might have been expected of him. He says, for instance, that it contains no allusion to the characteristic "*hujus*" of the Aquileian Creed* in connection with the "resurrection of the body;" whereas it contains two such pointed allusions.†
And the mere absence of that word from the heading of the paragraph in which this article is discussed is not more surprising than the absence of all heading from the corresponding paragraph in the work of S. Nicetas. Further, there are

* Vit. § 16.
† His comment is, "Summa perfectionis concluditur; et *ipsa caro, quæ cadit*, resurrectura erit immortalis, ut maneat." And in his introduction still more clearly: "Resurrectio tandem humani generis *in eandem carnem* in vitam æternam futura est."

passages in this "Exposition" which are neither epitomised nor in any way derivable from that of Rufinus, taking both as they now stand. I instance the concluding remarks of Fortunatus on "the Crucifixion," which are clearly borrowed from some other source than Rufinus, if not his own.* And there is a similar passage, unlike anything in the work of Rufinus, at the end of the next paragraph.† Again, Fortunatus never notices, or alludes to the existence of those words, "invisible" and "impassible," in the first article. Consequently, when Fortunatus, at the very commencement of his Exposition, tells the story of the formation of the Creed in fewer words than the "*Tra-*

---

* "Ideò crucifigitur, quia mortui eramus per pomum et arborem, ut denuò crux et Christus, id est arbor et pomum, per ipsam similitudinem nos a morte liberaret. Pomum dulce cum arbore." And the same of the two or three sentences preceding.

† "Et legatus Dominus, magis legatarius, pax inter partes extitit, et judices a livore dissolvit."

dunt majores" of the other, I am so far from thinking he was epitomising Rufinus, that I feel convinced he was expanding him,* and was expanded himself afterwards into the full-blown narrative with which Rufinus has been credited ever since. This, as the full-blown narrative *first* appears in S. Isidore, who became Bishop of Seville four years before Fortunatus became Bishop of Poitiers, but survived him by thirty years and upwards, to have been done at all, must have been done speedily: can it have been by S. Isidore? Let me begin by stating what put this into my head first. Setting this Exposition on one side, I searched through other works for the earliest mention of, or allusion to, the legendary story now found there; then

---

* What he says on "Credo in S. Spiritu" I take to be another expansion; and therefore marked "Sicut enim . . . cuncta sanctificans" . . . in a previous note as having been interpolated in § 35 of Rufinus. They are the words of Fortunatus, not his.

to name no more, with some colour—though inaccurately, as will be shown hereafter—who were contemporary with or lived after Rufinus. And he is himself the first, let it be said once more, who makes the Apostles in so many words authors of a Creed anterior to the Nicene. Lastly, that the style employed in dedicating this Exposition to Bishop or Archbishop Laurence "fidelissime Papa Laurenti," was still current, is shown from its employment in various letters scattered about the "Miscellanies" of Venantius Fortunatus addressed to bishops; and he was, as we have seen, of the same age with S. Isidore. Closer readings of history supply grounds for believing them to have been still more closely connected. Venantius, according to his biographer, studied at Ravenna, which Theodoric, King of the Ostrogoths, had so largely embellished and enriched as his capital,*

* See the glowing description of it by Gibbon, c. xxxix.

and then resided at Aquileia; from whence, some years before the Lombard invasion, he removed into France at the invitation of Sigebert King of Austrasia, whose marriage with Brunechilde, daughter of Athanagild King of Spain, together with her conversion from Arianism, he celebrates as a poet in the sixth book of his Miscellanies.

Their daughter Ingundis married back into Spain, and converted her husband, S. Hermenegild, at the cost of his life; but Reccared, his son, on succeeding to the throne abjured Arianism at the Third Council of Toledo, A.D. 589, thanks, as we are told by S. Gregory, to the influence of Leander, elder brother of S. Isidore, and his immediate predecessor in the See of Seville. Now, how much is known of the history of S. Isidore and his brother? Little, for certain, of their early life; still the general belief is that Severian, their father, Governor of the Province of Carthagena in Spain, was either son or son-in-law of the Ostrogoth King, Theodoric,* that he was exiled on account of his faith, A.D. 552, or thereabouts, and that S. Isidore was born in exile. Where this occurred has never been ascertained, though variously conjectured; but many years afterwards S. Gregory the Great met Leander at Constantinople during his own residence there, A.D. 578-84, and if they had not been acquainted before,† they continued friends from that time: so much so, that S. Gregory commenced writing his great work, called "Morals," on the Book of Job, at the request of Leander, and dedicated it to him when finished. What was Leander doing at Constantinople just then? "He had come," says the biographer of S. Gregory, "thither on business of the Visigoths as ambassador."‡ Had his family then got

* Areval. Proleg. ad S. Isid. c. 17 *et seq*.
† S. Gregory himself says elsewhere: " Dudum mihi in amicitiis familiariter functo,' . . . of Leander—Dial. iii. 31.
‡ Vit. i. 17.

back to Spain in the interim, or were they still exiles? It would not follow at all necessarily from his transacting business at Constantinople for his Spanish friends that he should have "come thither" *from Spain*. Had he been resident there, or in the vicinity, this alone might have determined their employing him to negotiate for them at the seat of the empire, as better acquainted with its usages and language than one who had never been there previously. To which add this further consideration. At the before-named Council of Toledo, A.D. 589, where Leander figured conspicuously, and his master abjured Arianism, it was the Creed and definition published *by the Fourth Council* that were professed; nor were the rulings of any General Council whatever, other than the first four, recognised in any way there by the bishops or by the king.*

---

* The king says indeed, incidentally, that he accepts all other Councils not at variance with

Had they forgotten the Fifth Council, held only thirty-six years before? If not, on what grounds could they have passed it over? Neither at Constantinople nor at Rome, by Patriarch John or by Pope Pelagius II., was respect for any Council insisted upon more just then, as Leander must have known well from S. Gregory. But there was just one district in Italy still where it had never been received, and was as persistently rejected as ever, and that district was Istria, of which Aquileia was, as we have seen, the principal town; and Istria, when Severian, the father of Leander and S. Isidore, was turned out of Spain, was and had long been subject to the Ostrogoths, his near kinsmen. After their overthrow by Narses, one of the first requests addressed by Pope Pelagius I. to their conqueror, A.D. 556, was that the "false Bishop" of

those four; but here he is speaking not of General Councils, but of Councils generally — Comp. can. ii.

Aquileia*—false merely, because persistently opposed to the Fifth Council—"might be turned out;" but Narses elected to leave Paulinus undisturbed;† and Paulinus held on there for twelve years longer at least, afraid of none but the Lombards. May it not have been in his diocese that Leander and S. Isidore passed the greater part of their exile? They would have certainly been treated there with all the respect due to the descendants of the great Theodoric: and the varied acquirements of S. Isidore, his knowledge of Greek and of Greek literature, so difficult to account for on the hypothesis of his having been educated in any part of a remote, and then re-barbarised country like Spain, would thus at once be explained. " Hispalensis" he would natu-

* Baron. A.D. 556, n. 10.

† See "Vit. Patriarch. Aquil.," in Muratori xvi. 7. He removed, A.D. 568, of his own accord to the adjacent island of Grado, " Lombardorum rabiem metuens," says Paul the Deacon: Hist. ii. 10.

rally be called from having died Bishop of Seville. Educated there, educated as he was, he could not have been. He may well have been educated, on the other hand, in schools that Venantius Fortunatus was just leaving, and in the laying of whose foundations such men as Boethius and Cassiodorus had been concerned. Istria being again in the line then taken to Constantinople from Italy— for people rarely went in those days by sea—S. Gregory may have made acquaintance with Leander in passing; and Leander, and even S. Isidore, may have visited Constantinople more than once before they finally returned to Spain. Residence, too, by the former in Istria would explain what may be called the Istrian bias of the Third Council of Toledo; residence there by the latter, the contemporaneous attention directed to the Aquileian Creed as by Venantius, so by S. Isidore. For here let me state clearly my contention to be, not that we are told anything about it in this Exposition absolutely fictitious, but that the addition of those words "invisible" and "impassible" to its first, and of the descent into hell to its fourth article, which I deny to have been in it in the days of Rufinus, had really been made there by this time, and both through influences obvious enough to appreciate when stated. The Ostrogoth dynasty was at all times more disposed to favour Arianism than orthodoxy;* and for both additions, as we have seen, the only precedents on record, in any formal profession of faith, had hitherto been semi-Arian. "*Invisible and impassible*," says this Exposition, "words added to our Creed on account of the heresy of Sabellius: the heresy called by our people the Patripassian, as it asserts the Father to have been born of a Virgin, and become visible, or suffered on the Cross." To

* See Gibbon, as before, on the reign of Theodoric, c. xxxix.

exclude, therefore, such impiety respecting the Father, our ancestors seem to have added these words, and called the Father "invisible" and "impassible." "Those who speak of the Father, Son, and Holy Ghost as the same person . . . we exclude with good reason from the Church, as they represent the incomprehensible and impassible Father at once comprehensible and passible through the Incarnation. Such are they who are called Patripassians by the Romans, and Sabellians by us," said the authors of the Macrostyche. "I believe in God the Father Almighty, invisible and impassible," says the Creed of Aquileia. "I believe in God the Father Almighty, invisible, unbegotten, and incomprehensible," said Count Pascentius, the Arian, to S. Augustine, being exactly what the authors of the Macrostyche had written to the bishops of Italy sixty years before. The Arians affected to be as much opposed as the orthodox to the Sabellians; and the Sabellians had been revived in France, Spain, and Italy by the Priscillianists. The Arians were for having the descent into hell inserted into Creeds: the orthodox would be reconciled to its insertion, as demolishing a favourite tenet of the Arians themselves. Both additions to the Creed of Aquileia, we may therefore, without hesitation, attribute to the effect of Arian influences in North Italy, subsequently to the establishment of the Ostrogoth kingdom in those parts.

And those who thus added to the Creed, would naturally seek to bring what a local celebrity like Rufinus had written on it into keeping with its enlarged form, and so bespeak equal antiquity for the whole. Quite possibly, they may have interpolated Rufinus to a much greater extent than this: transformed his work, in short, to what it now is. But of the two, it seems to me rather more probable that Venantius, from what he had read elsewhere, supplied the legendary tale, to the extent to which he gives it, as a kind of preface to his own " Exposition ;" and that S. Isidore having been asked by Archbishop Laurence to furnish him with a sound commentary on the Creed to take to his remote diocese— perhaps on the very ground that their joint friend and superior, S. Gregory, had obliged his own brother Leander similarly — borrowing this story from Fortunatus, whose writings he must have read, even if they had never met in Istria, and expanding it in its own fashion, incorporated it into the work of Rufinus then current, which, appropriated and retouched by himself, he finally dedicated and forwarded to the Anglo-Saxon Metropolitan, as furnishing him with all he wanted. Strange coincidence, should this prove the correct account of one of the first works printed at Oxford!

That this description of book-making was in high vogue then, and long afterwards, hardly needs any proof, except for those who never have made the literature of this period their study. The writings of S. Isidore and of S. Ildefouse, Archbishop of Toledo some thirty years later, are mainly constructed on this principle. Rarely naming their authorities, they string passages together from the Fathers, sometimes not in their entirety, but broken off purposely to be dovetailed as one, sometimes interspersed and glossed upon by remarks of their own. Sometimes you begin with four or five lines only from one writer, unnamed; then you have, without any warning, a long extract from another unnamed equally, whose views henceforth are preferred; then several sentences charged with a further idea, which you cannot discover at all in other authors; then a sentence of which one clause seems as much intended to betray its origin as the remaining clauses to conceal theirs. It is the most confusing literature to deal with that ever was penned. Let us hope that it was not designed to mislead. It is as perplexing to reconcile with chronology, as the different additions, in so many different styles of architecture, to our cathedrals. There is a treatise to which, as it will again be brought under notice further on, I may be allowed to refer here, simply for illustration. It has come down to us as a work of Alcuin, written at the request of Charlemagne, on the Trinity. It is, in point of fact, an adaptation of S. Augustine's work on the Trinity to the views then current;—exactly what, I contend, had been done by S. Isidore, or some contemporary, for this Exposition of Rufinus. That it could not have been all written by Rufinus as it stands now has, I think, been proved beyond dispute. That S. Isidore republished and dedicated it in its enlarged form to S. Laurence of Canterbury is a conjecture that I would not be understood to press for more than it is worth. Although next to nothing authentic has been preserved of S. Isidore beyond that he was brother of Leander, his predecessor in the See of Seville, and composed many works remarkable for their varied erudition and scholarlike style, nobody can read what he wrote, and call to mind what Spain then was, without feeling morally certain that he must have been educated elsewhere than in Spain. At that time there could have been no better schools anywhere than in North Italy, to judge from the literary achievements of those who were brought up in them or contributed to their foundation. And it is precisely to North Italy that the parents of S. Isidore would have been drawn naturally by their Ostrogoth connections when obliged to quit Carthagena. The monarch who expelled them from Carthagena must have been equally potent at Seville, and, indeed, throughout Spain, otherwise how could the conversion of all Spain from Arianism have been decided by that of King Reccared so soon afterwards?

Lastly, grant North Italy to have been the place where Leander and S. Isidore were brought up, and all that is authentic in their respective histories, is explained intelligibly, and much accounted for that is fictitious. S. Isidore dwells on the character of S. Gregory with the enthusiasm of one that had once known him;* but the story that he visited Rome during his pontificate is discredited not merely by his own silence, but by the fact that he is not so much as named in his letters. Even to Leander the Pope seems to have written but twice, and then rather as to one he had known formerly than with whom he was still intimate; and some people may fancy they can detect a certain reserve in his style, as though the reticence of the Third Council of Toledo on a subject of such urgent interest to him just then had not escaped him. He was rejoiced, of course, to hear that Spain had abjured Arianism: he

* De Vir. Illust. ad f.

would have been doubly rejoiced had it proclaimed its adhesion to that General Council which, in spite of all he could say or do, North Italy would not receive.

There is one more topic, in conclusion, not to be forgotten in favour of this hypothesis. Venantius Fortunatus had, as we have seen, studied at Aquileia. He seems to have been the first Western, literally, not of Aquileia, who treats of the descent into hell in expounding the Creed. That he carried it with him from Aquileia must be considered as certain as that it was not in the Creed there when Rufinus wrote. When even Venantius wrote, neither France, Spain, Africa, Rome, nor Milan had adopted it into their respective Creeds. Hence the author of the "Explanatio Symboli ad initiandos"—one of the many tracts on the Creed impudently palmed upon S. Ambrose by their authors or transcribers[*]—

[*] Printed by Mai (Script. Vet. Nov. Coll. VII. 157), but *without* saying of it, as he does of a letter

who must have seen the work of Rufinus in a more or less interpolated form, and often outstrips it in that direction

to S. Jerome, which he prints next, "I scarce doubt this being a genuine work of S. Ambrose." (Pref. r.) Another used to be headed "In Symbolum Apostolorum Tractatus," consisting of thirty-two chapters, and had the Apostles' Creed, word for word as now used, prefixed to it. The Benedictines, while rejecting this as a work of S. Ambrose, printed it in their Appendix as a tract "On the Trinity," without any Creed prefixed to it, and enlarged by three chapters. (App. p. 322.) Another appeared in the Roman Edition as "Sancti Ambrosii Episcopi Expositio fidei sive Symboli Nicæni contra Arium et Photinum Explicatio." This the Benedictines would not print even in their Appendix. Each of these tracts was printed as his at Rome on the faith of a "*vetustissimus codex.*" Just what the Cardinal pleads in behalf of the tract in question: "*Eam deprehendi in pervetusto Vaticano Codice.*" But then he had another reason for publishing it. The treatise "De Sacramentis," printed among the works of S. Ambrose, should have contained, he thinks, some such instruction on the Creed, but does not. And the MS. in which he found this tract contained also this treatise. But who has not heard of the feather that broke the camel's back? The Benedictines only printed this treatise among the works

himself, ignores this article. Gregory, bishop of Tours, and patron of Venantius when in France, prefaced his history with a solemn profession of faith, in which it is wanting. Nevertheless, S. Isidore, in arranging a formula for the fourth Council of Toledo some forty years after, follows Venantius, not Gregory. We have no proof that he corresponded with either; but supposing him to have been acquainted

of S. Ambrose to avoid giving any offence, loudly proclaiming their own doubts of its genuineness: on which see Cave, Hist. Lit. i. 263. And the idea of improving it by encumbering with a tract far more questionable was not, after all, quite as original as his Eminence seemed to think. "Enimvero non possumus satis mirari," say they (Prof. ad Tom. iii. p. 2, Ed. 1751), "tot libros atque sermones sancto Doctori suppositos fuisse, que ab *ejus ingenio, stylo, sæculo, penitus, abhorrent:* et quorum etiam nonnulli inter aliorum Scriptorum opera circumferuntur. Sed hoc admirationem nobis incutit multo majorem, quod malè feristi quidam homines *adeo illuserint fidei publicæ*, ut aliquas commentationes *quas Ambrosii non esse liquido prodebat prima lectio*, variis locis interpolarent, quo eas pro Ambrosianis securius liceret obtrudere," etc.

with the writings of both equally through the mother of King Reccared, who came from France, why should he not have followed the tradition of France rather than Istria? Plainly, some direct channel must have existed for Aquileian leanings and literature to have found their way into Spain to the extent they did—Aquileian literature, for S. Ildefouse had the "Exposition" of S. Nicetas as unmistakeably before him* as S. Isidore that of Rufinus: Aquileian leanings, already shown to have been exhibited in the Third and Fourth Councils of Toledo.— Now, had S. Isidore studied in North Italy, like Fortunatus, he would not fail to exhibit similar leanings; and then the simultaneous importation of this article of the descent into hell into Spain and

---

* De Cognit. Bapt., c. 33, where the last sentence of c. 13 of S. Nicetas de Symb. occurs word for word. In the same way the first sentence of § 14 of Rufinus occurs word for word, § 5, c. 30, b. i. of S. Isidore De Off. Eccl.

France is explained naturally. There is, of course, no necessity for supposing either him or Venantius conscious of its Arian origin. The re-publication of this Exposition of Rufinus, with additions and corrections, dedicated to Archbishop Laurence by S. Isidore, would go far to account for the *incognito* that it preserved so long, and for the diversities of title given to it when its authorship first began to be inquired into. Possibly the dedication to Archbishop Laurence may have been substituted for one by Rufinus himself, in which his own name occurred. A work by Rufinus may just as well have been supplied with a new preface as the translation of the work of another by Rufinus with a new ending. As was observed previously, the so-called letter of S. Clement to S. James contained, when it was translated by Rufinus, exactly twenty chapters, and no more. Twenty-four new chapters are tacked on to it in the edition of the pseudo-Isidore, and it is in the very first of these that the legendary tale now commencing this Exposition is epitomised. Nobody can fail to be struck by such a coincidence. It almost suggests a doubt how far S. Isidore may not have been here tampered with himself. In one case he has certainly been credited with a letter, some parts of which cannot possibly be his, as will be pointed out hereafter in treating of the Athanasian Creed; but in this instance the evidence both from his own writings and from the writings of S. Ildefouse, who was almost his contemporary, suggests that we need not go beyond him for anything contained in this Exposition as it now stands, any more than we can stop short of him. It is, accordingly, worthless for every purpose for which it has been usually cited as evidence till the seventh century.

CHAPTER II.

ON THE ROMAN CREED.

DIVESTED of its interpolations, we find the work of Rufinus in substantial harmony with that of S. Nicetas, as preserving the precise form of the Aquileian Creed in their day; the bishop in reality, testifying to its having advanced, as was natural, rather than receded, as his commentator was driven to infer, in the half-century between him and Rufinus. According to Rufinus, it ran thus:

1. I believe in God the Father Almighty:
2. And in Jesus Christ, His only Son, our Lord,
3. Who was born by the Holy Spirit of the Virgin Mary,
4. Was Crucified under Pontius Pilate, and buried:
5. Rose again the third day from the dead,

6. Ascended into Heaven, sitteth at the right hand of the Father,
7. From thence he shall come to judge the quick and the dead:
8. And in the Holy Ghost;
9. The Holy Church:
10. The remission of sins;
11. The resurrection of the body.*

Eleven articles in all. And what he says of it at starting† amounts to this: that it was one of the fuller forms of the Creed, compared with that of the Roman Church, in use then: all other Churches, as far as he could learn, having expanded their Creeds to exclude some novel teaching or

---

* S. Nicetas makes "life everlasting" its last article, supplies the word "Catholic" before "Church," and by explaining "Church" to be "the congregation of Saints," prepared the way for this as a distinct article. If he omits "et sepultus," he supplies "mortuus." And in fact each of his apparent omissions here are supplied in his other treatises: *e.g.*, "et sepultus" in Rat. fid. c. 6; "Unigenitum," De Sp. c. 14; and, "Dominum Nostrum," De div. appell., c. i. For "*hujus* carnis resurrectionem," as he was addressing his catechumen, he says "*tuæ*."

† § 3.

other advanced by heretics, while the Roman Church, never having bred heresy, still adhered to the ancient custom of making her catechumens rehearse the Creed publicly, so as to be heard by all present, that none might ever be able to add a word to it unchallenged by their predecessors in the faith, who would of course remember what they had recited themselves.

In the days of Rufinus, as everybody knows, the only public occasion on which any Creed was ever used in any Church, was at the administration of the Sacrament of Baptism, for which the candidates, or catechumens as they were called in consequence, had been prepared by previous instruction. Part of this instruction consisted in delivering them a Creed by word of mouth, to be learnt by heart and afterwards rehearsed publicly by them on presenting themselves at the font. The act of the bishop or priest in delivering it to them was called "Traditio Symboli," and he explained its parts to them simultaneously; their act in rehearsing it in the same form was called "Redditio Symboli:" and this, whether it took place, in conformity with the forty-sixth Canon of Laodicea,[*] on "the fifth day of the week"—of the week before Easter, that is—or any other, for the day varied in different Churches, everywhere formed part of the baptismal ceremony. The Creed of a Church in those days, accordingly, was the Creed employed in its office for baptism, and no other. As Eusebius said of that of his own See, in reciting and distinguishing it from that of the Nicene Fathers: "It was what he had received from the bishops preceding him, both when under catechetical instruction and on receiving bap-

[*] As Johnson (Vade Mecum ii. 117) translates "That those who are to be enlightened" (or baptized) "ought perfectly to learn the Creed," (compare the language of Canon 7,) "and rehearse it to the bishop or priest on Maundy Thursday."

tism."* Similarly, the Creed of the Church of Jerusalem has been preserved to us in the catechetical lectures on it by S. Cyril; the Creed of the Church of Aquileia in this Exposition of Rufinus, being what, as he tells S. Jerome, he had learnt as a catechumen himself: the Creeds of the Churches of Ravenna, Turin, and Africa were what SS. Peter Chrysologus, Maximus, and Augustine commented upon, in homilies that are still extant, orally to their hearers, to be repeated by them afterwards at their baptism. Just what S. John Cassian said of another form.† " The Creed then, O heretic, whose text I have been reciting "—most unfortunately he stops short at the article on the Incarnation—" is that of all the churches in some sense—the faith of all being one— but peculiarly that of the city and church of Antioch: the Church in which you were brought forth, instructed, and re-

* Soc. i. 8.
† De Incarn. vi. 6. The Creed is given c. 3.

generated. The faith of this Creed it was that conducted you to the font of life, to the regeneration of salvation, to the grace of the Eucharist, and Communion of our Lord." And S. Epiphanius of both forms which he has given at length in his " Ancoratus :"* of the shorter one first :

" Continue, then, O faithful and orthodox, to preserve this holy faith of the Catholic Church, as she, the one holy virgin of God, received it from the Apostles of our Lord, and so ought ye to instruct each of the catechumens coming to the sacred laver, not merely to rehearse their faith to their own sons in the Lord, but to say in words, as doth our common Mother : ' We believe in one God,' " etc.

Then of the longer one, which he says had been adopted in consequence of the heresies invented between the Nicene Council and the publication of his treatise

* C. 118-121.

—precisely what Rufinus says of the fuller forms in the West—

"On this account both we and you, and all orthodox bishops, and in a word the whole Catholic Church, to meet the heresies that have arisen, agreeably with the faith promulgated by those holy Fathers, enjoin those coming to the sacred laver especially, to repeat, and say as follows: 'We believe,'" etc.

Later, the form promulgated at Constantinople, and confirmed at Chalcedon, became the baptismal Creed of one local church after another in the East, as the acts of the Council of Constantinople under Mennas, A.D. 536, testify; the Fathers of three previous Councils which are there quoted—at Constantinople, Jerusalem, and Tyre, A.D. 518—all calling it the Creed used at their own baptisms, and which they used in baptizing others.[*] And this form, as everybody knows, has

[*] Mansi, viii. pp. 1044, 1052, 1059, 1063, 1070, and 1079.

been handed down to us at full length; and with the exception of the gloss of King Reccared on the Procession, is still recited in our churches after the Gospel, word for word as it stood then. There are, therefore, these four Western, and five Eastern forms of the Creed at least, extant word for word as they were used during the fourth and fifth centuries in the churches whose catechumens were taught them. What they contained, as well as when and where they were used, is matter, not of inference or conjecture, but of plain fact. Either they are recorded at full length, as being peculiar to this or that church, or else commented upon article by article for the benefit of this or that church's catechumens. Has it been ascertained, or is it ascertainable, what the Creed of the Church of Rome was then, upon equally clear evidence? It would have been so ascertained long since, had authors thought less of perpetuating conjectures, than of investigating

ON THE ROMAN CREED.

facts. Professor Heurtley must excuse me for referring to him again as an instance of this; his manuals, drawn up with so much care in all that concerns himself, would have been worth twice what they are, had he followed others less implicitly by half. Voss and Usher, unquestionably, must always be quoted with respect on every subject they handled; but the liturgical discoveries of Muratori, Mabillon, and Martene, to name no more, had not been made when they wrote; and they would have been the last to ignore them, could they have seen them. One of their conjectures, in default of direct proof, had been, that the Creed of the Church of Rome was ascertainable from this Exposition of Rufinus. Professor Heurtley, accordingly, sets down a form —his fifth in order—which he heads thus: "Symbolum Romanum ex Rufini commentario:"* and then describes, " as

---

* "De Fide," etc., p. 31. Walch had given it in the same terms.

exhibiting, on the whole, the normal text of the Western Creed of the fourth and fifth centuries." That his description is at variance with his heading, will be shown presently: let us examine the justification adduced by him for his heading. "The Creed expounded by Rufinus is that of the Aquileian Church. He notes, however, as he proceeds, sundry discrepancies between this Creed and that of the Church of Rome: so that we thus obtain the text of the Roman Creed of his day, as well as that of the Aquileian."* *Sundry discrepancies* — my readers will, perhaps, hardly credit me when I tell them they will find but two such noted in all; and neither, in all probability, by Rufinus himself, as has been shown above. But this is a point on which I will not insist here. Taking his treatise as it now stands, the first discrepancy noted in it between the two Creeds

---

* "De Fide," etc., p. 29.

relates to the Aquileian addition of those two words, "invisible and impassible," which it says are "wanting in the Creed of the Roman Church;" the second to the "descent into hell," which it says is wanting there likewise.* As no other discrepancies are pointed out, Professor H. assumes the two Creeds must have been identical in all other respects, save where the Aquileian differs from all other Creeds, in asserting "the resurrection," not "of the body," merely, but "of this body:" which is a hasty inference, as we shall see. Of the descent into hell, Rufinus went on to say, that this article was as little known to the Eastern Churches as to the Roman. As he had not said the same of those words "invisible and impassible," we must, if we accept the Professor's reasoning, assume that the Eastern Creeds contained them. Again, as to that other statement of this Exposition, on which I remarked at starting: "As is

* De Fide, p. 122.

also said in the Creed,* 'And of His kingdom there shall be no end:'" what are we to infer from hence, that this article was the Aquileian and the Roman Creeds? The fact being that it was common to neither. Walch, to be consistent, endeavoured to apply the same principle to other Creeds, that Professor H. has applied exclusively to that of Rome. For besides the two discrepancies noted in this Exposition between the Aquileian and the Roman, he saw there were two likewise noted in it between the Aquileian and the Eastern Creeds. One of them has been discussed already: "the descent into hell," which no Eastern Creed ever contained: the other had reference to the commencement of the Creed, which in all Eastern forms sets out with belief "in *one* God, and in *one* Lord Jesus Christ." Walch, therefore, constructed an Eastern Creed † on the

---

* "De Fide," etc., p. 136.
† Biblioth. Symb. p. 38. The Roman is p. 37.

ON THE ROMAN CREED. 93

assumption of the Eastern and Aquileian Creeds being identical, except where their discrepancies had been set down by Rufinus; and the result was that he produced a form as unlike any of the Eastern Creeds extant, as can well be conceived :* save that it begins as they do; but is in all other respects as much too contracted, as the form assigned by Professor H. to the Church of Rome is too diffuse. Professor Heurtley has so far more colour for his heading, as the form assigned by him to the Church of Rome is proved directly by the treatises of SS. Peter Chrysologus, Maximus, and Augustine to have been in all other respects what he describes it to be, " the normal form of the *Western Creed* of the fourth and fifth centuries:" only that it is not

---

* In a subject of this kind I would not willingly resort to the ridiculous; but I cannot help likening this attempt to putting a bonnet on the head of a person otherwise dressed as a man, and then declaring him to be in female garb from head to foot.

therefore proved to have been that of the Roman Church. In the absence of any direct proof to the contrary, we might, to be sure, consider ourselves free to infer this; but, as I have said already, Rufinus himself intimates in express terms that such was not the fact: "Other Churches," he says, "had made certain additions to their respective Creeds; but in the Roman Church this had *not been done*. For there the candidate for baptism had never ceased to rehearse the Creed publicly, just as he had been taught it, and the addition of a single word would have been instantly noticed by the baptized of former years." In other words, the Creed of the Roman Church had not been added to, but retained its pristine simplicity: being identical with what had been used in administering the Sacrament of Baptism there from time immemorial. If, therefore, the baptismal office of the Roman Church of those days is extant, so is its Creed. We are thus brought to the liturgical discoveries of which I have spoken.

Muratori's "Liturgia Romana" contains three "sacramentaries" or "rituals" of the Roman Church, called after three Popes, SS. Leo I., Gelasius I., and Gregory I., their respective compilers or revisers, not authors, as Sir W. Palmer shows;* and Mabillon's "Museum Italicum" contains as many as fifteen short "orders" or "uses" of the same Church; but of these we may dismiss the last five from consideration on account of their lateness. I am not aware that any comparative analysis of these collections on any particular subject has yet been made: still less on that of the Creeds. At all events, what Gavanti, and after him Merati,† has written on the Apostles' Creed can only be characterized as so much rubbish, based on spurious evidence. It is on this head, and on this head only,

* Orig. Liturg. vol. i. § 6.
† Thesaur. ii. § v. c. 3.

that I profess to have tested these collections myself, and proceed to give my results.

Unfortunately, the first part of the Leonine Sacramentary seems to have been lost—at least it has not been printed—and with it whatever baptismal office this Sacramentary contained. Still, I expect to be able to prove the baptismal offices of the next to have been as old. Pope Gelasius I., in fact, being separated by little more than thirty years from S. Leo, almost equal antiquity might seem bespoke for the sacramentary bearing his name as a whole. But as our copies of it contain some later additions that we can detect, it is possible that they may contain others also to which we have no clue. Muratori's copy, for instance, contains an addition to the Canon of the Mass which we know from unexceptionable sources[*] to have been made by

---

[*] Palmer, as before. "Hanc igitur oblationem," etc.

S. Gregory. This copy, therefore, cannot have been in existence before the seventh century, and possibly not then: as in the office for Good Friday* a blessing is asked not only for the Roman but for the Frank empire. At the same time, quite possibly, this may have been interpolated into the existing copy; for, on another occasion,† only the Roman empire is prayed for, as in Muratori's copy, though not in Migne's,‡ of the Gregorian. Should it not follow from these accounts, that no greater antiquity can be claimed for the Gelasian Sacramentary than the Gregorian, as we have them? However, I am concerned only with their baptismal offices, and not with theirs by themselves either, as I said before, but read side by side with such

* " Respice propitius ad Romanum, *sive* Francorum imperium."—Liturg. Rom. i. 561.

† Prayers "in time of war."—Ib. 727.

‡ Muratori tells us his edition is from a Vatican MS. Migne's is evidently from a MS. of later date.

of the "Roman orders" published by Mabillon as contain any.

Now, it so happens that in the Gelasian Sacramentary we have two baptismal offices: one for Easter, and one for Whitsuntide, which were precisely the "two seasons" which S. Leo pronounced "legitimate;" while S. Gelasius prohibited administering baptism, except in cases of illness, at any other.* And in both offices the part relating to the Creed is identical, and runs as follows:

"Before pouring water over him"— such is the direction to the officiating minister in the first office—" you ask him the *words of the Creed*, and say: 'Dost thou believe in God the Father Almighty?' He answers, 'I believe.' 'Dost thou believe also in Jesus Christ His only Son our Lord, born, and suffered?' He answers, 'I believe.' 'Dost thou believe also in the Holy Ghost: the holy Church: the remission of sins: the resur-

* Bingham, xi. 6, 7, with the notes.

rection of the body?' He answers, 'I believe.'"

"*You ask him the words of the Creed*" —of the whole Creed then in use; for otherwise the catechumen would have been imperfectly questioned about his faith. " This was the " *redditio symboli*," says Mabillon,* " which Amalarius affirms

---

* Liturg. Rom. ii. 999, note. Martene (De Ant· Eccl. Rit. Lib. i. c. 1; Art. xiii. § 13) calls this "Interrogatio de fide;" thus apparently, though not expressly, distinguishing it from the " redditio symboli" which he had explained already (Art. xi. § 18.) Nor is Bingham more explicit. And there are passages: *e.g.* Ferrand, Ep. ad Fulgent. quoted by Bingham (x. 2, 10,) and S. Aug. Confess. viii. 2, quoted by Martene (ibid.) which seem to indicate that the "redditio symboli" consisted in the rehearsal of the whole Creed *in public* by each catechumen. On the other hand, even Martene, when treating of the "redditio symboli," notices that there is a rubric of the Gregorian Sacramentary preceding the prayer headed " *ad reddentes*," which runs as follows: " Dominus papa post *pisteueis;*" and on which he says: " Est autem *pisteueis* vox Græca πιστεύεις, id est, credis? quia interrogationes symbolum reddentibus factæ incipiebant." Now, anybody who will be at the pains of looking

took place, according to the Roman order, on Holy Saturday." "And this," adds Bingham,* "was always to be made in the same words of the Creed that every Church used for the instruction of her catechumens;" just as is done still in the

through his collection of baptismal offices (Art. xviii.) will see that in each case the interrogatories are longer or shorter, as the particular Creed then in use was long or short. (Orders iii. and vi. have the longest of all; orders iv. and xii. in one place follow the Roman use, but the Gelasian Sacramentary; orders v., x., xi., xii. in one place, and xvi.-xxi. the Roman use, but the Gregorian with additions. The rest have merely the first words in each case.) And further, that in *all the more ancient* of these services the recital of the Creed at length, even on the day of baptism, is ordered to be by the *priest alone*, as in the Gelasian: "Inde verò dicis symbolum, impositâ manu super capita ipsorum;" which same Creed is in the seventh of the Roman orders published by Mabillon expressly stated to have been the Niceno-Constantinopolitan; as in the tenth of those published by Martene likewise; though in France it was usually that of the West.

* XI. 7, 8. Perminius "De Sing. Lib. Can. Scarap." in Migne's Patrol. lxxxix. p. 1035, seems decisive on this head.

Church of England.* In the Gregorian Sacramentary there was no baptismal office for Whitsuntide seemingly, but only for Easter; and in this we have the same Creed again, word for word, save that "Maker of heaven and earth" has been inserted in the first article after the word "Almighty," and "Catholic" after the word "Church." Of the "Roman orders" published by Mabillon, only the first, which speaks of "the custom of bowing the knee for King Charles,"† and therefore cannot all of it be older; the seventh, which bears considerable resemblance to the office for baptism in the Gelasian Sacramentary; and the tenth, which Mabillon assigns to the eleventh century, contain any baptismal office at all; and in that of the seventh the Creed is not given complete. In that of the first and tenth the Creed of the Gregorian Sacramentary

* See the Three Offices for Baptism in the Book of Common Prayer: "Dost thou believe," &c.
† § 24. This has been reprinted by Muratori, ii. 974 *et seq.*

reappears, word for word, amplified only by "life everlasting" for its last article.

Such, therefore, were the exact dimensions of the Creed of the Roman Church for several centuries—say from the fifth to the tenth—on the showing of its own service-books; just what, I think, Rufinus, rightly construed, should have prepared us to expect. He represents it as of all Creeds the most elementary and least added to; and what is the baptismal Creed of the Gelasian Sacramentary but this? Compared with the Aquileian, given a few pages back, it will be seen that they agree, word for word, in the two first and four last articles with a single exception—a mere question of a pronoun—and that their entire difference consists in what is intermediate, relating to the Incarnation, which in the Roman is curtly summed up in two words, "born and suffered." On this head the contemporary Creeds of Aquileia, Turin, and Ravenna, to say nothing of the East, supplied what was not then, and for long afterwards, in the Roman; and anticipated so far the teaching of S. Leo. Hence, when S. Leo speaks, in his celebrated Epistle to Flavian, of "the universality of the faithful professing their belief in " God the Father Almighty, and in Jesus Christ His only Son, our Lord, Who was born of the Holy Ghost and the Virgin Mary," he is as certainly quoting the exact words of the baptismal Creed of his own Church in the two first sentences, as he is borrowing from other Creeds in the third. And when the words, "Maker of heaven and earth," "Catholic," and "life everlasting," were added to the Creed of his Church, as in the Gregorian Sacramentary, they had existed already for centuries in the Creeds of Jerusalem, Cyprus, and Constantinople, to say nothing of the West. As articles are reckoned in the Tridentine Catechism, it contained no more than eight in its original, and but nine in its enlarged shape; for out of the three additions made to it in the Gregorian Sacramentary, but one, "life everlasting," imports a new article. Hence, further, when S. Leo says in another letter—one to the Empress Pulcheria,* on which I must dwell again presently—" Forasmuch as the short and perfect confession of the Catholic Creed, which is marked by the sentences of the twelve Apostles in the same number, is supplied with celestial armoury to that extent, as to be able to decapitate all heretical opinions with its own sword alone;" whatever be the Creed of which he is here speaking, he cannot possibly mean that of his own Church, for the number of the Apostles exceeded that of the articles in the Roman Creed then by one-third; and for centuries afterwards by one-fourth. Never, in short, till it had been supplemented from other Creeds sufficiently, would the two numbers square.

* Ep. xxxi. ed. Migne.

Such, then, are the simple facts of a case on which so much romance has been written, and is still current. Of all the Creeds of those days the Roman could least pretend to have been composed, as even now the Tridentine Catechism maintains solemnly,* by the twelve Apostles. It was literally the shortest of all existing Creeds; distinguished from all other Western and Eastern professions equally, by the extreme brevity with which the Incarnation was expressed in it; and from all Eastern, in common with all Western, in that it commenced with the verb in the first person singular, instead of the first person plural—" I believe," not " we believe;" and asserted belief in " God," not in " one God." And hence those words of S. Ambrose, if he really wrote them, or rather if the letter addressed by him and other bishops to Pope Siricius originally contained them—" Let them believe the Creed of the Apostles,

* Pars. i. c. i. § 2, 3.

which the Roman Church ever guards and maintains inviolate"—which I doubt extremely, from the abruptness of their appeal, isolated alike from anything that precedes or follows them*—they can refer to no other.

---

* Ep. xlii. ed. Migne. It is a letter to thank the Pope for his promptitude in condemning heretics, particularly Jovinian, whom they proceed to refute. "Sed de viâ perversitatis produntur dicere, virgo concepit, sed non virgo generavit. Quæ potuit enim virgo concipere, potuit virgo generare: cùm semper conceptus præcedat, partus sequatur. Sed si doctrinis non creditur sacerdotum credatur oraculis Christi, credatur monitis angelorum 'Quia non impossibile Deo omne verbum.' Credatur symbolo Apostolorum, quod ecclesia Romana intemeratum semper custodit et servat. Audivit Maria vocem angeli," etc. All the rest of the letter is in continuation of this and other proofs from Scripture; and there is no hint anywhere what that Creed contained. It so happens that with the pseudo-Ambrose, *e.g.* the author of the "Expl. Symb. ad initiandos," this is apt to be a pet point. "Quoniàm symbolum Romanæ ecclesiæ nos tenemus;" and again, "Hoc autem est symbolum quod Romana ecclesia tenet, ubi primus Apostolorum Petrus sedit, et communem sententiam eò detulit," &c. (Patrol. xvii., App. ii. p.

There is yet one more question relating to the Creed of the Roman Church to be settled before we conclude. The letters of S. Leo to Flavian and Pulcheria were written at different times; that to the Constantinopolitan Patriarch before, that to the Empress after, the Fourth Council. But even before the meeting of the Fourth Council, exception had been taken by the friends of Eutyches to a passage which has been already quoted from the earlier letter, because the Creed appealed to there by the Pope commenced differently from that of Nicæa. "Why should he not have said 'in one God, and one Jesus Christ?'" they asked; to which Vigilius of Thapsus replied, that "at Rome, long before the Nicene Council came together, from the age of the Apostles down to his own, and during the pontificate of S. Celestine, whose orthodoxy they allowed, the Creed had ever been *so* delivered to

1155.) His zeal, possibly, may have led him to insert it here.

the faithful." So delivered*—in other words, with the "one" before "God," and "Jesus" omitted, which the Nicene Creed supplied. After the Council of Chalcedon, S. Leo never, as far as I can find, appeals to the Creed of his own Church again, but always to the Creed of Constantinople or Nicæa. Was it that he deferred to the Eutychians or to the Fourth Council? Of the Fourth Council we know that it was attended by a greater number of bishops than any previous Council, and that it passed a canon, distinguished from other canons in general by being appended to their definition of faith, and declaring under severe pains and penalties, that, in future, there should be but one Creed allowed for public use: viz., that of Constantinople and Nicæa combined. To this canon the Pope was

* This passage is adduced by Bishop Bull, Ind. Eccl. Cath. vi. 2, to prove the ante-Nicene origin of the Roman Creed, which of course it may; but *not what* that Creed *contained*, beyond what is here stated.

unhesitatingly pledged on the spot through his legates; but afterwards, in consequence of his determined opposition to the prerogatives claimed for the Constantinopolitan See by another equally famous canon passed in the teeth of his legates, he was reported adverse to the rulings of the Council in general by its opponents, and movements were set on foot in various parts of the empire for its revision. He had to exert all his influence to prevent these from taking effect; and accordingly seems to have felt called upon, in future, to be all the more explicit in declaring his acceptance of its dogmatic decisions without reserve, and all the more particular in appealing to its Creed. Thus, in the very first of his epistles to the new Emperor, his namesake, he says of its "rule of faith"—by which he means its Creed—"that having been promulgated by Divine inspiration,[*] it was incapable of improvement by sub-

[*] Ep. cxlv. ed. Migne.

traction or addition." He repeats this again and again in other letters.* In his last letter but one to the same Emperor, he recites the Nicene Creed proper at full length, to point out the harmony between it and his own doctrine.† With the monks of Palestine he expostulates for having "forgotten the saving Creed and confession they had recited before many witnesses on receiving baptism."‡ Their baptismal Creed was then, and had long been the Creed of Constantinople, as will be brought out more fully further on. Singularly, this, of the three Creeds named by him, alone contained *exactly twelve articles:* the Nicene Creed proper, exclusive of its anathemas, only containing eight, like the Roman. As, therefore, for other reasons, we might expect that in writing to the Empress Pulcheria, he would be careful, wherever insisting upon Creeds, to appeal to this, the Creed of the city

* See Ep. clxii., for instance, to the same.
† Ep. clxv. 3.   ‡ Ep. cxxiv.

where she ruled and resided, in preference to any other; so for this additional reason, when we find him declaring of the Creed to which he appealed that it contained "the sentences of the twelve Apostles in the same number," we cannot but infer that he could mean no other.

I have said that a canon was appended to the definition of the Fourth Council ordering that, in future, the Creed of Nicæa and Constantinople combined should be employed in every public ceremony, to the exclusion of all others. The Acts of the Third, or Council of Ephesus, had contained a decree to the same effect as regards the Creed of Nicæa, though less solemn in form. By the succeeding Emperors, Basiliscus and Zeno, even when opposing the Fourth Council, its Creed is regularly spoken of as the sole creed allowed, "in which they and all their subjects and progenitors everywhere had been baptized and professed their faith."* It received similar testimony from the Councils of Constantinople, Jerusalem, and Tyre, as we have seen in the next age.† Later, only by another generation, we have the Emperor Justinian declaring, in a formal edict, that "the Fathers of Ephesus and Chalcedon, besides wholly following the same holy Creed in condemning the errors of Nestorius and Eutyches, anathematised all who delivered a definition of faith—that is to say, a 'creed' or 'lesson' to any presenting themselves for holy baptism, or coming over from any heresy whatsoever other than the one propounded by the 318 holy Fathers"—who met at Nicæa—"and expounded by the 150 holy Fathers," who met at Constantinople.‡

---

* See particularly the Encyclic of Basiliscus, Evag. iii. 4, and the Henoticon of Zeno, ib. 14. Peter of Alexandria says the same further on in his letter to Acacius, ib. 17.

† Above p. 87.

‡ His edict, or "Confession of Faith," against the three Chapters.—Mansi ix., 557.

After this interpretation of its meaning by the Prince of Jurisconsults, there can be no room for doubting what were the restrictive constructions put upon this canon by contemporaries, while having been passed at Ephesus as well as Chalcedon, it was as much upheld by the opponents as by the supporters of the latter Council: a convincing proof how very generally it was then observed. Again, the matter-of-fact way in which the joint Creeds of Nicæa and Constantinople are connected in the edicts of Basiliscus and Zeno with the administration of baptism proves that in this respect its provisions must have been obtained in many churches long before they became law for all. And with this correspond not merely those passages from S. Epiphanius above quoted, where this Creed appears prefaced by the statement that it was what all catechumens should be taught to rehearse, but also the well-known statement of Theodore the reader, who flourished in the early part of the sixth century; that till A.D. 517, or thereabouts, this Creed used to be recited in church "on one day of the year only—viz., on Maundy-Thursday, at the catechisings by the Bishop.* It seemed difficult to reflect on these facts without coming to the conclusion that what had thus become law for the empire must have become law, sooner or later, in Rome, too. Nor was this conclusion otherwise than abundantly strengthened by considering further the conspicuous part played by the Roman Bishops at each of the Councils of Ephesus and Chalcedon, and the outspoken and often-repeated adhesion of S. Leo to the doctrinal decrees of the latter. Even with no other data to build upon than these, there was, surely, some ground for inferring that the Creed promulgated at Chalcedon must have been at one time received into the baptismal offices of the Roman Church,

* II., p. 32.

either in connection with, or to the abandonment of what had been used there previously. Coming to the Gelasian Sacramentary, therefore, with this surmise, I was agreeably surprised to find it not only confirmed there to the letter, but supplemented in more ways than one, as I shall explain in detail. It has been shown, some pages back, that both at Easter and Whitsuntide, for what is called the "Redditio Symboli," or rehearsal of the Creed by the catechumens in the act of receiving Baptism, the form given in the Gelasian Sacramentary was a form consisting of eight articles only, and that this form, in reality, was and had been the Creed of the Roman Church downwards till then. But the administration of Baptism came last in a train of preliminary ceremonies, among which that of the "*Scrutinium*," or examination of candidates, ranged over several weeks previous. The office for this is given in a place by itself in the Gelasian Sacramentary, and to understand it properly we must go to the seventh of the Roman "orders," as printed by Mabillon, which consists of this exclusively, with directions for its performance. There are several other copies of it, indeed, extant besides these two. "Ita ut intelligamus," as Muratori says, "illo usam fuisse Romanam ecclesiam,"* not, however, that it was peculiar to the Roman Church except in this form, as might be shown from Martene.† In the Roman Church, then, "notice" was given of this "examination of candidates" on the second day or Monday of the third week in Lent‡, in the following words: "The day of examination, dearly beloved, in which our candidates are taught heavenwards, is at hand. Be pleased, therefore, to be care-

* Lit. Rom. i., 531, note Comp. Mabillon, Mus. Ital. ii., 75.

† De Ant. Rit. Eccl. Lit. i., c. 1, Art. ii. *et seq.*

‡ "Denuntiatio pro scrutinio, quod tertiâ hebdomadâ in Quadragesimâ secundâ feriâ initiatur."

ful to attend on the fourth day of the week next ensuing, at the third hour,* that we may, by the help of God, be able duly to perform this heavenly mystery, by which the devil, with his pomp, is destroyed, and the gate of the kingdom of heaven set open, through Jesus Christ," etc. There were seven such examinations in all, of which that on Easter Eve was the last: and at the end of each of the first five the day of the next was announced, showing that, with the exception of the first and the last, the days for holding them were not necessarily the same every year. But it would seem to have been always at one of the examinations held in the fourth week that two solemn lections—one from Isaiah, the other from the Epistle of S. Paul to the Colossians—were read, and the commencement of each of the four Gospels expounded, "*in aurium*

---

* This is the reading of the seventh Roman "Order," and, no doubt, the correct one.

apertionem," for the opening of the ears, in each case. And then followed the "*traditio symboli*," or delivery of the Creed to the candidates, " prefaced as follows :"* "Dearly beloved, ye that are to receive the Sacrament of Baptism, and be begotten a new creature of the Holy Spirit, embrace with all your heart the faith by which, believing, ye are to be justified, and, having your minds turned by true conversion to God, the Illuminator of our souls, draw near and receive the Sacrament of the Evangelical Creed, inspired by the Lord, instituted by the Apostles; brief in words, to be sure, but vast in mysteries, forasmuch as the Holy Spirit, who dictated these things to the masters of the Church, composed, for saving purposes, a faith with such eloquence and such brevity that what you must believe and keep always before you

* "Incipit præfatio symboli ad electos : id est, antequam dicas symbolum, his verbis prosequeris."

should neither be above your comprehension nor fatigue your memory. Learn, therefore, the Creed with attention, and that which we deliver to you, as we received it ourselves, inscribe, not on any corruptible substance, but on the pages of your heart. This, then, is the beginning of the confession of faith which ye have received."*

What is the Creed which follows? "In what language do these candidates for baptism confess Christ?" asks the presbyter, and the answer is, "In Greek." Addressing the Acolyth, he continues: "Declare their faith in the form in which they profess it." And the Acolyth, placing his hand on the head of one of the children, repeats the Niceno-Constantinopolitan Creed, which is given at length, in Greek, word for word as it had been promulgated at the Fourth General Council. "You have heard the Creed in Greek, dearly beloved," resumes the presbyter; "hear it in Latin. In

* Liturg. Rom. i. p. 539.

what language do these confess Christ?" and the answer having been, "In Latin," he bids the Acolyth "declare their faith as before," and again the same Creed is repeated at length in Latin, word for word, as it had been in Greek.

Thus, in the earliest extant Office for baptism of the Roman Church, the Creed delivered to her Catechumens was the Niceno-Constantinopolitan emphatically, the only Creed *then* in general use, be it remembered, whose Articles amounted to twelve, neither more nor less; and it was of this Creed, and no other, that her clergy were told to declare, by way of preface to it, that it had been "inspired by our Lord, instituted by His Apostles, dictated by the Holy Ghost." Her earliest Sacramentary contains no such glorification of the shorter Creed in which her catechumens had been instructed till then. This shorter form, to be sure, she retained so far as to limit the questions to be asked of the catechumens at the font, and consequently their answers to its more simple terms, as before. And, indeed, in the instruction which follows the rehearsal of the Niceno-Constantinopolitan Creed, that Creed is, perhaps, as much interpreted by the shorter form as the shorter form by it. This, at all events, is what is then put into the mouth of the presbyter.

"Such is the sum of our faith, dearly beloved; these are the words of the Creed, not made by the wisdom of human speech, but arranged by the true reason that is from above, being what nobody lacks the ability to comprehend or retain. Here the power of God the Father and the Son is declared equal and one. Here the only-begotten of God is set forth born according to the flesh of the Holy Ghost and Virgin Mary. Here His crucifixion, burial, and resurrection on the third day is preached. Here His ascension above the heavens, and sitting on the right hand of the Majesty of the Father, is confessed; and

His coming again to judge the living and the dead proclaimed. Here the Holy Ghost is professed inseparate from the Godhead of the Father and the Son. Here, lastly, the calling of the Church the remission of sins and resurrection of the flesh is clearly taught. . . . . You have thus, dearly beloved, arrived at a knowledge of the before-named Creed of the Catholic faith; now go and, without changing a word of it, learn it by heart." The rest is irrelevant. In all that relates to the Father, Son, and Holy Ghost, this epitome represents rather the fuller than the shorter form. The remaining Articles are plainly epitomised from the shorter form, into which "life everlasting," as we have seen, had not yet been inserted, which is, doubtless, the reason why that truth is not noticed in this epitome.

That the Roman should have so far retained her old traditionary Creed, even in adopting that of the Fourth Council in exchange for it so far, becomes intelligible enough, if we apply the remark of Rufinus to the circumstances of those times. Education was not likely to have been improved or extended at Rome by the invasion of Attila, which had preceded the Fourth Council by forty years; and the public rehearsal of the Creed by candidates for baptism might have provoked a burst of fanaticism had it embodied so much as a word which the mass of the faithful had not been taught themselves in their day. Accordingly, what was "delivered" to the catechumens in private, forty years after the Fourth Council—supposing this change to have commenced with Pope Gelasius—was the Niceno-Constantinopolitan Creed: what was "rehearsed" by them in public immediately before receiving baptism was the same with what we find used in the Church of Rome still. And in the epitome of the Creed put into the mouth of the presbyter charged with instructing them, there is a clear reference to both forms, as has been shown.

It may be asked, possibly, what proof there is that the prefatory remarks preceding "the delivery" of the Creed had been composed expressly for the Niceno-Constantinopolitan Creed on its introduction; and had not likewise preceded the delivery of the shorter form till then. This might be admitted; and yet even so the fact would remain that the Roman Church had as little hesitation in asserting of the Creed of the Fourth Council that it had been inspired by our Lord; instituted by the Apostles; dictated by the Holy Ghost:" as of her own: plainly showing in what sense they had formerly been said of her own. But after all, this is mere hypothesis. The Gelasian Sacramentary contains the oldest baptismal office extant of the Roman Church. Accordingly we may assume, for all that appears to the contrary, that this preface, as it stands there, was expressly composed for the Creed to which it there serves as an introduction, namely that of the Fourth Council. And further, anybody comparing what is said of the Creed in this preface with what S. Leo says of it in his letter to the Empress Pulcheria, will hardly dispute the probability that the author of this preface borrowed from that letter of S. Leo. But that S. Leo must have been discoursing on the Creed of the Fourth Council in that letter has been already proved.

Afterwards, when the Gelasian and Gregorian Sacramentaries were introduced into France by Charlemagne and his successors, either from the custom of chanting the Creed of the Fourth Council at Mass having already prevailed there for some time, or else from national repugnance, this Creed was not generally substituted at the " traditio symboli " before baptism for that of the West. Martene says he found it in a pontifical of Saltzburg: and it occurs in a pontifical of Poitiers given by him at length: and in the tenth of his orders further on. On the other hand, that which had formed the preface to it in the Gelasian Sacramentary appears in several of his other Orders as a preface to the Creed of the West, by that time lengthened into twelve articles, and supposed to have been actually composed by the Apostles. Hence, so far from this preface having been accommodated in the Gelasian Sacramentary to the Niceno-Constantinopolitan Creed, it was, on the contrary, borrowed from that ritual in France to be accommodated to the Creed of the West, whose "institution by the Apostles" was beginning to be maintained, according to the then current legend, in a far different sense from what these words had borne when predicated of the Creed of the Fourth Council. The Gallican prefaces themselves, it should be noted, so far as they have been preserved, had contained no sort of allusion to this supposed authorship of the Western Creed.*

On the morning of baptism, similarly, where the Niceno-Constantinopolitan Creed is directed in the Gelasian Sacramentary to be recited by the Priest alone, the earlier Gallican Orders published by Martene † contain a direction to the same effect, with this exception, that it is the Western Creed which they prescribe. Yet, when the candidates are called upon to answer for themselves at the font, the questions put to them are taken from the Gelasian or Gregorian Sacramentaries; in other words, it is the Roman Creed in which they are then called upon to profess their faith. The questions in Orders IV. and XII. in one place are from the Gelasian; in V., X.-XII., and XVI.-XXI., they are from the Gregorian, more

---

* See those given in Martene, Art. xi., from the "Ancient Gallican Missal."

† Art. xviii.

or less added to, as was remarked in a previous note. As regards the more recent Orders, the only change to be noticed in them is, that on the morning of baptism the rubric, instead of directing the Western Creed to be recited by the priest alone, enjoins him to call upon all present, or at least the sponsors, to recite this Creed with him. The rubrics of Order XVI., and several others following, are to this effect.

Such, then, were the modifications which the Roman office for baptism underwent in France, when introduced there by Charlemagne; and they are the more to be noticed, because they found their way eventually to Rome itself, equally displacing there what they had displaced in France, and are to this day observed in all churches of the Roman obedience. Witness this rubric of our own times in their baptismal service: " The priest as he proceeds to the font, says, *along with the sponsors*, in a loud voice"*—not the Niceno-Constantinopolitan in accordance with the Gelasian Sacramentary—but the Western Creed, in accordance with the semi-, but only semi-Romanised Gallican offices of the eighth and ninth centuries. Afterwards, as in those same Gallican offices, the candidates are questioned respecting their faith at the font in the exact form prescribed by the Gregorian Sacramentary, with its latest additions, and differing only from that of the Gelasian in being more full.

Thus in the existing office for baptism of the Roman Communion, we have conclusive testimony both to what was originally the Creed of that Church, and to the vicissitudes which it has undergone since. Previously to the days of Pope Gelasius, it must have been either identical with the form preserved in his Sacramentary, or else more simple; more simple, because whatever changes it has

* " Golden Manual," p. 676.

undergone since then have been in the way of addition; identical, because the directions there given to the priest at the font,—" You ask him the words of the Creed "—are direct testimony to what its exact dimensions were then. The candidates, had they rehearsed continuously what they were then asked in three separate questions, must have said:

> I believe in God the Father Almighty;
> And in Jesus Christ His only Son our Lord, born and suffered;
> And in the Holy Ghost, the holy Church, remission of sins, and the resurrection of the body.

This is, again, precisely what they would say still: save that they would insert " Maker of Heaven and earth " at the end of the first article; and " Catholic " before, and " the Communion of Saints " after the word " Church " in the middle of the third, and " life everlasting" at the end. The second article has remained to this day intact.* Of these four insertions, the two first appear in some copies of the Gregorian Sacramentary without the two last; in other, and therefore probably later copies, with the two last as well. Hence this Creed is virtually recited by every catechumen of the Roman Communion still, word for word as it stood in the seventh or eighth century. But, further, previously to the days of Pope Gelasius, or at all events of the Nicene Council, this Creed must have been the one "delivered" to catechumens during their "scrutiny," as well as professed by them at the font. It is of course possible that the Creed "delivered" to them may have been at one time that of the First Council: still, before then it must have been as certainly the Roman, as it was afterwards the Niceno-Constantinopolitan. And the

* "Golden Manual," p. 678; but two glosses have been introduced into the English most gratuitously.

Niceno-Constantinopolitan it remained, doubtless, till this was in turn displaced by the Western Creed subsequently to the introduction of the Roman Order into France. In the Gregorian Sacramentary the office which should contain it is simply wanting; for that the "scrutiny" before baptism existed at Rome then and long afterwards in full vigour, is proved by its adoption in France, according to the Roman manner of conducting it, in the ninth century, with the preface to the Creed, and in several cases the Creed itself, unaltered from the Gelasian Sacramentary. Thus we see that the Roman Church has at one time taught her catechumens one creed, and at another another, in preference to her own: though she has always questioned them on her own at the font; in other words, she has admitted, in retaining her own, that it had been improved upon in other churches. And hence, finally, we see that if, according to the statement of Sir W. Palmer,* who derived it from Mabillon, "all the sacramentaries (in France) were taken from the Roman Order, from the time of Charlemagne:" there were several particulars, notwithstanding, on which the Roman Order had in turn ultimately to yield to the Gallican, even on as high a point as the Creed.

* Orig. Liturg. i. p. 146.

CHAPTER III.

FROM CREEDS VARIABLE TO CREEDS FIXED AND UNIFORM.

THERE are two or three more points relating to Creeds in general—*public Creeds*, I mean, *solely*—that need elucidating to make the whole subject intelligible. First and foremost, there is the distinction which might have saved endless confusion had it had justice done to it previously, between creeds oral and written. If it was over-stated by Le Brun, it was underrated assuredly by Muratori in opposing him.[*] The facts of the case are simple enough. The germ of all creeds lay in the baptismal formula;[†]

[*] Liturg. Rom. Diss. c. 1, *ad fin*.
[†] S. Matt. xxviii. 29: "Go ye make disciples of all nations, baptizing them in the name of the

and their employment at any public service was for centuries limited to the baptismal ceremony. As long as this was the case, the creed of each Church was oral essentially, and therefore not fixed or uniform. It was oral, it is shown to have been oral, for these reasons. It was not merely peculiar as regards other churches; but, firstly, different versions of it prevailed at different times in the Church whose creed it was; secondly, different versions of it were given of it by writers of the same age; and thirdly, occasionally by the same writer. Professor Heurtley, for instance, culls a shorter version from one place, and a longer from another, of the Creed of Jerusalem, in the catechetical

Father, and of the Son, and of the Holy Ghost," which is exactly S. Cyril's shorter form of the Creed: "I believe in the Father, and in the Son, and in the Holy Ghost; and in one baptism of repentance." Heurtley, "De Fide," p. 3. Whence, doubtless, S. Nicetas (Symb. Expl. ad init.): "Hanc regulam fidei Apostoli a Domino acceperunt, ut in nomine Patris et Filii et Spiritus Sancti omnes gentes baptisarent."

lectures of S. Cyril.* A longer and a shorter form of the Baptismal Creed used in the churches of Cyprus, is given by S. Epiphanius.† S. Augustine in his different Expositions of that of the African Churches, varies the wording of it several times. "This last article," says Rufinus, on the Aquileian Creed, "which asserts the resurrection of the body, concludes its summing of the perfection of the whole with succinct brevity:" showing how it ended in his time. It ended, not many years after his death, according to S. Nicetas, with "life everlasting." Even the Roman Creed is shorter in the Gelasian, than it is in the Gregorian Sacramentary; indeed, there are scarce two copies extant of either, that are word for word with each other. Thus, even after it had been committed to writing, and commented upon, it fluctuated, and was liable

* " De Fide," pp. 3 and 9.
† Ib. pp. 11-15.

to change from still being oral as well.

It may be said to have been oral *ex officio*, so long as it stood for public use nowhere but in the baptismal office; this being one means of concealing it from those who had not received or not been pronounced fit for baptism. " The catechumens having been dismissed," says S. Ambrose, " I delivered the Creed to the '*competentes*' in the baptisteries of the church."* And Rufinus: " It is further reported to be a customary thing in civil wars, that because their arms, language, method, and manner of fighting are the same: therefore every general, to prevent fraud, should give his soldiers a distinct symbol—which in Latin is called *signum*, or *indicium*—that if one met another, of whom he had reason to doubt, by asking him the symbol, he might discover whether he was friend or

* Ep. xxxiii. ad Marcellin., quoted by Bingham, x. 2, 10, note.

foe."* Great pains, accordingly, were taken in early times to conceal the Creed from the uninitiated or unbaptized, on which Professor Heurtley,† as well as Bingham ‡ enlarge.

But it continued oral also for another reason. "Nobody commits the Creed to writing," says S. Augustine, "that it may be read: rather let your memory serve for a manuscript, that you may be able to repeat without any chance of forgetting, what has been delivered to you with so much pains."§ And Rufinus: "The last of their ordinances was that these things should not be written on paper or parchment, but retained in the hearts of the faithful, that it might be certain that none had learnt them from reading, an accomplishment which even infidels are now and then wont to ac-

---

* § 2. Bingham, x. 3-1.
† Harm. Symb. p. 32, note.
‡ X. 5, 9.
§ Serm. ad Catech. § 1; printed by Heurtley, "De Fide," etc., p. 85.

quire, but from Apostolic tradition."*
And this reason would remain in force, for what it was worth, long after the ages of persecution had passed. On the other hand, the Creed ceased to be oral, and took a permanent form by degrees everywhere, from being incorporated into various other services besides the baptismal, after which it also became fixed and uniform even there. How this took place will appear presently, when account has first been taken of another and a commoner distinction: viz. that between the baptismal creeds of the East and West. The baptismal creeds of the West all converged, and at last met, in what has been since called "the Apostles' Creed:" the baptismal creeds of the East lay at the foundation of, and at last were lost in, the Niceno-Constantinoplitan, on its becoming the Creed of the whole Church. Yet this in the Greek has preserved, and still exhibits, all the idiosyn-

* "De Fide," p. 105.

crasies of the one group as much as that of the Apostles in our own tongue those of the other. As though by preconcerted arrangement, all the Eastern commenced with "*We* believe in *one* God:" all the Western with "*I* believe in God." This was their archetypal characteristic. And they had others, as they were gradually developed on either side. For instance, " the Communion of Saints," one of the latest additions to the Western Creed, looks almost as if it had been inserted in direct preference to the " one baptism " of the Niceno-Constantinopolitan : at all events, profession of the latter never obtained in the West, nor of the former in the East. "He descended into hell," similarly, never found place in any Eastern and *orthodox* formula ; nor " Whose kingdom shall have no end," in any Western of any kind. But they agreed on both sides in having been all oral originally, and then had their developments stopped by becoming oral no longer. The Creed of the First Council, by whomsoever it was composed, is, as I have said, cast in the Eastern type : and corresponds too closely with that of the Church of Cæsarea preserved by Eusebius, not to have been borrowed from it to some extent.* At the same time, there is no reason to think that the Nicene Creed proper ever figured in any public service : still less displaced the baptismal Creed of any local Church, unless, possibly, the African: after its reception into what is called the African code :† thus accounting for the " Credimus in unum Deum ... et in unum Dominum J. C," of Facundus, Bishop of Hermiane, in the next century, which Professor Heurtley cannot explain.‡ Nor had even the Niceno-Constantinopolitan Creed any such effect, till it was promulgated by the Fathers of the Fourth Council along

* Heurtley, " De Fide," etc., pp. 4, 5.
† As canon 137.
‡ Harm. Symb. p. 51.

with their definition, which had a canon appended to it forbidding under severe pains and penalties the employment of any other creed in any way for public use. This, as has been already noticed, had been preceded, as far as words go, by a similar enactment of the council of Ephesus, in favour of the Nicene Creed proper. And both enactments owed their origin clearly to the same phenomena: the diversities and constantly shifting forms of the creeds in use, and the multiplication of new creeds. But the canon of the Third Council was not, as far as we know, followed by any practical results; the canon of the Fourth Council, on the other hand, effected two radical changes almost immediately, which have never since been dropped. The first of these was the application of the strict letter of the canon to the Baptismal Creeds hitherto in use in the East, and their consequent abandonment in every local church for that of the Council. The second was the insertion of this Creed into the liturgy or Communion Service, immediately after the Gospel, as now: a step which, if not actually prescribed by the canon, proved highly conducive to its strict observance.

The proofs of both changes have been anticipated;[*] and it must certainly be ascribed to their joint operation, not only that the Niceno-Constantinopolitan Creed has been the only Creed employed for public purposes in the East ever since, but also that it is to this day recited there without exception, in public and private, word for word as it stands in the acts of the Fourth Council. All other creeds having been prohibited for public use by this canon, it found its way into various other services gradually besides the baptismal, and so became stereotyped in all alike: the oral character of the Baptismal Office being itself at length merged in the written character of the rest. Obedience

[*] Above, pp. 111-112.

to this canon in the West, where Rome exercised patriarchal jurisdiction, was regulated by private judgment alone, or by policy. She accepted it herself to some extent, and for some time; but left others entirely free to please themselves. She incorporated the Niceno-Constantinopolitan Creed into her baptismal ritual in one place, retaining her own in another. But she would not insert it in her liturgy, where no creed had previously been rehearsed. Further, when it suited her policy, she violated the canon in more ways than she had ever observed it; first, by substituting the Western, wherever she had inserted the Niceno-Constantinopolitan Creed, in her Baptismal Office; and, secondly, by at last electing to insert the Niceno-Constantinopolitan Creed in her liturgy: not, forsooth, as it had been transcribed into her Office for Baptism from the acts of the Fourth Council word for word by the author of the Gelasian Sacramentary, but as it had since been interpolated by two crowned heads, Reccared and Charlemagne. Then, finally, to conceal her tergiversations, she discarded it altogether from her Baptismal Office.

That the other churches of her Patriarchate dictated their own course to her in the end, instead of conforming to hers, is as plain, historically speaking, as anything can be. Let me review their proceedings chronologically, even at the risk of repeating myself. First: their use of the Niceno-Constantinopolitan Creed in the liturgy or Communion Service. This, as has been observed already, was enjoined by no part of the enactments of the Fourth Council. The Council ruled that no other creed should in future be compiled or employed for public use but the Niceno-Constantinopolitan: not that this creed should become inseparable from every public service, or be inserted in any services where no creed had been used hitherto. Still there can be no doubt that its insertion in the Liturgy must have been to some extent suggested or favoured by the decrees of the Fourth Council, inasmuch as this took place, shortly afterwards, in every Orthodox Church throughout the East. But in the West notoriously the first to order its insertion in the Liturgy was the Spanish King, Reccared, on his abjuration of Arianism at the Third Synod of Toledo, A.D. 589, forty years, in round numbers, after the Fifth Council, and 140 years after the Fourth. Now, if we turn to the Acts of this Synod, which extend over several pages folio, and abound with dogmatic statements, all affirmed to be in harmony with the faith of the first four Councils, one of the first things that strikes us is, that they contain no mention whatever, much less any such formal acceptance of the Fifth Council, the nearest to it of all in point of time. And the moment we try to account for this omission we are reminded that the

Acts of the Fifth Council had been all but unanimously condemned in the West, and that there was a large party still in North Italy that repudiated them. Next, if we recall some striking coincidences before noticed in connection with King Reccared and his friends: *e.g.* that his own conversion is explained by the fact of his mother having been a French princess; that at the time of her marriage Venantius Fortunatus, the well-known poet, was also the most esteemed theologian at her father's court; that he (Venantius) had been educated at Aquileia, where, there is good reason to think, Leander, Archbishop of Seville, and ecclesiastical president of this Synod, though his junior by many years, may have been his schoolfellow; and that at Aquileia, finally, schismatic opposition to the Fifth Council waxed hottest just then. If we put all these circumstances together, we may possibly discover in the Acts of this Synod a declaration of Aquileian leanings, rather than of pure orthodoxy. And then, thirdly, the fact that the First Synod to decree the insertion of the Niceno-Constantinopolitan Creed in a Western Liturgy should have been the first, likewise, to exhibit it in the interpolated form which it now bears—viz., with the "*Filioque*" clause—may be explained satisfactorily by supposing that the copy of the Acts of the Fourth Council, produced at this Synod, had been obtained from a city whose bishops had been, till quite recently, subject to a heterodox ruler, and were now schismatics.

This explanation may be thought far-fetched, but from the twofold fact attempted to be solved by it there can be no escape. It is as undeniable that the Niceno-Constantinopolitan Creed was not inserted in any Western Liturgy till it had been interpolated, as that its insertion in the interpolated form it now bears in all Western liturgies was ordered in the first instance by crowned heads.

"The Holy Ghost," said King Reccared to his assembled bishops, "ought to be confessed equally by us, and taught to proceed from the Father and the Son, and be of one substance with the Father and the Son." He then, shortly afterwards, recited the Niceno-Constantinopolitan Creed at full length before them all, with those words added: "And from the Son."* The abjuring prelates, when it came to their turn, anathematised with marked emphasis "those who do not or cannot believe that the Holy Spirit proceeds from the Father and the Son." Then the King, addressing the Council again, ordained of his royal authority that, "To give stability to the recent conversion of his people, all the Churches of Spain and Gaul"—Gallia Narbonensis, *i.e.* comprehending the provinces of Languedoc, Provence, and Dauphiny—"should observe this rule: namely, that at every time of the sacrifice, before com-

---

* Mansi, tom. ix. p. 977 *et seq.*

municating in the Body and Blood of Christ, the most holy symbol of the faith should be recited in a loud voice by all, according to the custom of the Eastern Fathers." And forthwith a canon was passed by his bishops to this effect: "That in all the churches of Spain and Gallicia the symbol of the faith of the Council of Constantinople be recited *according to the form of the Eastern Churches*, so that it be chanted in a loud voice by the people, before the Lord's Prayer is said." The bishops professed that they were for reciting the Niceno-Constantinopolitan creed in their respective dioceses "according to the form of the Eastern Churches:" in practice they conformed to that of their King.

And their precedent speedily became law in Spain. At all future Synods of Toledo down to the seventeenth, A.D. 694, inclusively, this creed, whenever it was recited at all, was invariably recited with the interpolation authorised by King

Reccared; and from Spain it was probably carried into France, and, perhaps, England, in this shape by the end of the next century, though no notice seems to have been taken of it, nor any particular stress laid upon it, till the Synod of Frankford, A.D. 794, upwards of two centuries after its first promulgation in Spain. Up to that time, for aught we know to the contrary, it may have been supposed word for word with the Creed promulgated by the Fourth Council. But the Synod of Frankford met, as everybody knows, in avowed hostility to the Seventh General Council, whose Acts had been published seven years before, and since confirmed by the Pope. And among them was the Creed promulgated by the Fourth Council in its original shape. That this Creed was attacked at Frankford, and attacked expressly, for not containing the interpolation authorised by King Reccared, appears from a work called "The Caroline Books," written either by the theologians of Charlemagne or by that monarch himself, which, having been submitted to the Synod, was approved there, and contained a vigorous denunciation of each and all of the decrees of the Seventh Council, including its creed. Its creed, said the author of this treatise, was defective, because not sufficiently explicit upon one point. What could its members mean by such reticence? "Assuming them to be orthodox on the point in question, still we are bound to consider them on the verge of error *for having neglected to make profession of their orthodox sentiments.*"* And the Synod of Frankford proved that it endorsed this reasoning by adopting the interpolated creed as its own. More deliberate schism was never committed by any synod. Nor was this all. Notice of its proceedings, with a copy of the work approved by it, having been sent to the reigning Pope, he not merely vindicated every part of

* Lib. iii. c. 8 in Migne's Patrol. tom. xcviii.

the teaching of the Seventh Council that had been attacked with his own pen, but intimated that the penalties appended to the definition of the Fourth Council were incurred by all who impugned its Creed.

One might have supposed that such determined action as this on the part of the Pope would have compelled the supporters of the interpolated Creed to retrace their steps, but they took little heed of his words. Even Paulinus of Aquileia, the most considerable of all the Caroline bishops, in presiding over a Synod of Friule two years after that of Frankford, not merely reiterated his adhesion to it, but apologised for it, on the ground that, as the Second General Council had enlarged the Creed on the subject of the Holy Ghost considerably beyond what the first had laid down: so, to refute those heretics who said that the Holy

---

* Patrol. ibid. p. 1272. See the remarks on all this in my pamphlet, "Is the Western Church under Anathema?" pp. 33-6.

Ghost belonged to, and proceeded from the Father alone, those words had subsequently been added, "And from the Son." When, and by whom they were added, indeed, he particularly shirks stating; and, in conclusion, he passionately contends for the orthodoxy of all who professed either form of the Creed. "How catholic those Fathers who, grounded in faith unwavering, have confessed the Holy Ghost to proceed from the Father! How glorious those, likewise, who have confessed Him to proceed from the Son as well!"* I ask the reader to take particular note of this position of the Aquileian patriarch, for a reason that will appear further on. It has been maintained again and again on both sides since the schism between the East and West commenced, but it must be held to have been rejected on both sides equally, as each side to this day accuses the other of error on the Procession. However, this by the way. Here let us confine

* Mansi, tom. xiii. p. 835.

our attention exclusively to the fact that the first time such a compromise was suggested it was by Paulinus of Aquileia, and that till his death, or for ten years more, no further discussion of the subject is recorded to have taken place. But almost immediately after his death it was provoked in the very heart of the East by some Frank monks, and, to judge from their narrative, it seems more than probable that their course had been traced out for them beforehand by their Imperial Master. As soon as their proceedings had attracted sufficient notice, they wrote from Jerusalem, where they were staying, to the Pope, then Leo III., to say that one John, of the monastery of S. Sabas, had accused them of heresy, and tried, in consequence, to get them put out of the Church of the Nativity at Bethlehem on Christmas Day; that the priests and the people had assembled on the Sunday following over against the Sepulchre— that is, in the space between it and

Calvary—and questioned them on their faith and creed. They replied that their faith was that of the Roman Church, but that they knew that in their mode of saying the doxology, the hymn "Glory to God" and the Lord's Prayer, they used some expressions that were not found in the Greek; and that in the Creed they spoke of the Holy Ghost as proceeding from the Son as well as the Father, which was the reason why John had called them heretics. This explanation of theirs had, indeed, failed to give satisfaction, or, at least, allay the excitement. But they defended themselves to the Pope by saying that *one of their number*, Leo, *before leaving the West, had heard the Creed so sung in the Imperial Chapel;* that *Charlemagne had also made them presents of a Homily of S. Gregory and the Rule of S. Benedict, and his Holiness of a dialogue, where the same expression occurred: and that it was so, moreover, in the Creed of S. Athanasius.* Still, they cannot but acknowledge that it was not so read in the Greek form of the Creed. And, therefore, they beg his Holiness to ascertain from the Emperor whether the Creed was not sung in his chapel, as they had stated, and then instruct them how to act for the future.*

The Pope wrote to Charlemagne requesting him to intervene for their personal safety, but without the remotest allusion of any kind to the point on which they had asked his directions. If he enclosed their letter entire, it was without comments; if he accompanied it with "a profession," which he said he was sending them, "of the orthodox faith, which should be held stedfast and inviolate by all members of our Holy Catholic and Apostolic Church," this was not merely forwarded to the Emperor "for perusal," but evidently was meant

* "Christendom's Divisions," ii. 71-2, corrected in some respects. It is given by Neale in full: "Eastern Church," vol. ii. 1155-9.

to be transmitted through him. And there can be very little doubt but that it has come down to us as he revised it rather than as his Holiness penned it, for this simple reason. It speaks of the Holy Ghost as proceeding from the Father and the Son in one place, and as proceeding equally from Both in another. And at the end of the whole we read: "Him that believeth not according to this faith, the Holy Catholic and Apostolic Church condemns." This, I stated in a former work, "was the strongest and most explicit declaration that had emanated from any Pope hitherto in favour of the views then prevalent in the West on the Procession."* And this, I have become convinced since from what followed, could never have been made by Leo III. then. Charlemagne was no sooner in receipt of these despatches than he convened a Synod A.D. 809, at Aix-la-Chapelle, to discuss the very point on which the monks had

* "Christendom's Divisions," p. 72.

consulted the Pope with so little success, that of the interpolated clause in the Creed, and deputies were sent from thence to Rome with a long letter, as from himself, in which the procession of the Holy Ghost from the Son is not only proved, but distinguished carefully from His temporal mission. "So I think, so I hold," was the exclamation elicited from the Pope on hearing this letter read. Would he not have added: "So I wrote myself in the profession which I asked his Majesty to read and send on for me," had his own profession been as explicit on the subject, as it is in the form which it now bears. Or had it been received from him in the form which it now bears, would the Emperor have failed to notice the harmony between it and his own views in his reply? Such a letter as was brought by these deputies to the Pope from the Emperor, must imply surely, that either the Pope had not explained himself previously to the Emperor on the subject of which it treats, or that his explanation had not been considered satisfactory. On the point relating to the Creed indeed, the Emperor was as silent as the Pope had been; but the deputies came purposely to press it upon the Pope by word of mouth. Their conference was a long one, spread over two days. Towards the end of it, one of the deputies asked: "As I understand, then, your Holiness orders that the clause in question be first ejected from the Creed, and then afterwards be lawfully and freely taught and learnt by any one, whether by singing or by oral tradition?" To which the Pope replied: "Doubtless, that is my desire: and I would persuade you by all means so to act." If this was impossible they might give up using the Creed at Mass altogether; and this he counselled, in conclusion, as the better plan: "Let the custom of singing that Creed cease in the Palace, since it is not sung in our Holy Church." As Charlemagne had adopted the custom of *chanting* the liturgy from Rome some years before, the not *singing* the creed was in both places, then, equivalent to the not using it. Finally, the Pope, to give publicity to his determination of preserving the creed unaltered in his own church, had a silver tablet made with two plates or compartments, and the creed engraved in Latin on one, and in Greek on the other: in either case without those words, " and from the Son." And this was by his orders affixed to the " confession " or shrine of S. Peter in the church of that name. S. Peter Damian writes of it in the eleventh century that it was then seen in front of the shrine of S. Paul.*

This looks as if it had been removed from S. Peter's, where it had hung originally, to S. Paul's Church, though

---

* Opusc. xxxviii. Do Process. Sp. S.: " Beatus etiam Leo Papa in argenteâ tabulâ, quæ ante sacratissimum corpus beati Pauli Apostoli videtur, erectâ," etc.

there are said to be relics of both Apostles in each now. And what indeed could be more likely than that it should have been removed, if, as is stated by Berno, the interpolated creed had been incorporated into the Roman liturgy just before then. Berno, besides being at Rome when it happened, was, as I pointed out to Archbishop Manning,[*] a liturgical writer, and actually then engaged in a work on the Mass; so that "he would naturally be very particular in his inquiries when he came to Rome, of all places, how things were done there." And his account is that, "up to that time, the Romans"—that is, the Church of Rome generally—"had *in no wise* chanted the Creed after the Gospel; but that the lord Emperor Henry would not desist till he had persuaded the lord, Pope Benedict, to let it be chanted at Mass."

Now, the only creed then chanted at

[*] "Church's Creed or the Crown's Creed," p. 10.

Mass in the West being this interpolated creed, there was no necessity for Berno to explain what creed it was which the Emperor pressed upon the Pope. Similarly, there can be no more for me to prove that it was this creed: as it is this Creed and no other which is used in the Roman liturgy to this day. Crowned heads authorised its interpolation; crowned heads decreed its insertion in the Communion Office, where it has ever since stood. On both points Rome conformed to the West, not the West to Rome.

Further: the Western Creed was adopted in time by Rome: not the Roman Creed by the West. This is another of those facts which merely want stating with sufficient fulness to be indisputable. I have demonstrated already what the Roman Creed was—in fact, still is—and shown it to have been much more distinct from all other Western forms of the Creed, than they from each other. Western forms varied, mainly because they were oral; the Roman, though oral, was protected by constant recital in public from change. Western forms, as they ceased to be oral, became fixed and uniform, and were finally merged in what has long been, and is still, called the Apostles' Creed: the Roman, comparatively crystallized from the first, remains a distinct form to this day. Both forms as we have seen, exist side by side in the Roman Office for Baptism now in use: where the priest is directed to repeat the Western Creed along with the sponsors in proceeding to the font; but to interrogate them afterwards merely to the extent of the Roman. When and how the Western Creed got incorporated into the Roman ritual has yet to be shown. Western Creeds, I have said, had a genius and mould of their own, and were far from being copied servilely from the East, still less from Rome: the Roman Creed being merely part and parcel of the same family with themselves. It must be remembered, indeed, that our earliest specimens of public creeds begin with the fourth century, and that we can hardly compare them one with another in any fairness before the fifth. Subject to this proviso, then, we may say of the Western Creed in general, that the additions made to it after this date, which were purely Western, and not copied, were the following:

1. The article, "Born by the Holy Ghost of the Virgin Mary:" enlarged to, "Conceived by the Holy Ghost, born of the Virgin Mary."
2. The article, "Crucified under Pontius Pilate and buried:" to, "Suffered under Pontius Pilate, was crucified, dead, and buried."
3. The article, "Sitteth on the right hand of the Father:" to, "Sitteth on the right hand of God the Father Almighty."
4. A new article, viz., "The Communion of Saints," was inserted immediately after that of the Church.

Similarly, the additions made to them after this date, which were copied—*must have been copied*, as they existed in other Creeds previously—were the following:

1. "Maker of heaven and earth:" copied from Eastern Creeds.
2. "He descended into hell:" copied from the Third Sirmian and other semi-Arian Creeds.
3. "Catholic" between the words "holy" and "Church:" copied from Eastern Creeds.
4. "Life everlasting:" copied from Eastern or African Creeds.

None of these additions are found in the Gelasian Sacramentary; and but three, viz., 1, 2, and 4 of the second set in the Gregorian: all copied from the East. Number 4 alone of the first set has been received into the Roman Creed since then: and this came to it from the West.

How each of these additions passed, from being local and oral at first, into general acceptance finally, will be seen to most advantage by selecting one of them as a specimen. Every candidate for baptism in Africa was asked, according to S. Cyprian, whether he believed in everlasting life, and remission of sins through the Church. But how the Baptismal Creed of the African Church ended in the days of S. Augustine, is extremely doubtful on his own showing. At one time he comments on it, as though it ended with "the resurrection of the body;" at another, as though it ended with "everlasting life." Every local creed being then oral, as I explained before, it was not always recited word for word in the same form even by the same person. But it can hardly have been from Africa that "everlasting life" was imported into the creeds of the West. Rufinus affirms in express terms that the last article in the creed on which he was commenting was "the resurrection of the body"—"*ultimus iste sermo*"—as he therefore calls it. And this was likewise the last article in the Roman Creed, when the Gelasian Sacramentary was composed. There is one creed, indeed, of earlier date, which ends with "everlasting life;" and this by Professor Heurtley is headed: "Symbolum Romanum a Marcello Ancyrano Julio Papæ traditum," A.D. 341.* I must be allowed to express my extreme surprise, to read in a work, designed more particularly for the benefit of students, anything so groundless and misleading—misleading, as S. Epiphanius is cited in a note for this title,† which he not only never suggests, but discredits in every word he says; groundless, as I shall not require much space to show.

Marcellus was a bishop of the Eastern Church, deposed from his See of Ancyra, in Galatia, by the Arians, in a Synod held, A.D. 336, at Constantinople. He was restored, in company with S. Athanasius and others, first in a Roman Synod under Pope Julius, A.D. 342, and ulti-

---

* "De Fide," *et seq.*, p. 24.
† Hær. 52, al. 72.

mately by the Council of Sardica, A.D. 347. All we know of his movements for certain, between A.D. 336 and 347, is, that he was personally present at each of the Synods that restored him, and that he spent on one occasion a year and three months in Rome. What we know of his character even from his friends is not reassuring as to his orthodoxy, or straightforwardness in general. S. Athanasius himself once intimated, with a smile, to S. Epiphanius, that if he said nothing against Marcellus, it was not that he had much to say in his favour. He then, according to S. Epiphanius, before leaving Rome on the occasion referred to, whenever that was, addressed a letter to Pope Julius, enclosing a profession of his faith, written, as he says, with his own hand; being what he had learnt, been taught from Holy Scripture, and preached in church, and of which he always kept a copy by him. What should those words mean? That the profession he enclosed was the Creed of the Roman, which he never so much as hints it was,* or of his own Church? Of his own Church most assuredly: what else could be gathered from them? How should Marcellus have learnt, been taught, or preached any other creed at Ancyra than the Ancyran? At the same time most certainly *this*, his profession was *not: at least, in the shape it then bore*, which was purely Western. Accordingly, what S. Epiphanius suggests—and what few people surely would have much difficulty in believing—is, that it was concocted by the deposed prelate for the occasion: for the purpose, that is, of clearing himself. And this, again, may have been the reason why it was sent,

* " Romanum quidem se symbolum tradere nunquam dixit Marcellus," says Walch, whom Professor H. quotes in a note: Harm. Symb. p. 24. Had he said so, adding that it was *also* the Baptismal Creed of his own Church, his credit certainly would not have stood high with the Pope.

and not presented to Julius in person, Marcellus being in Rome still. Further, it would appear from the same author that Marcellus employed more professions than one; and that in dealing with Easterns the Creed in which he professed his faith was that of Nicæa. This profession of his is extant as well as the other; and was being employed by his disciples in their own justification, when it was placed in the hands of S. Epiphanius. It is headed, " Writing of the faith of Marcellus." Putting them both together, we see plainly that he aimed at being an Eastern to the Easterns, and a Western to the Westerns. The only question that remains is, how he managed to succeed so well in this last respect? And here geographical considerations may help us. How would Marcellus get most naturally from Ancyra, which lay in the heart of Asia Minor, to Rome? First, the proceedings instituted against him at Constantinople would be likely to bring him thither, and detain him there for some time. Next, as his condemnation there preceded his acquittal at Rome by six years, if he came to Rome previously to his acquittal, and his stay in Rome was limited to fifteen months, he cannot have moved westwards very rapidly, and may have spent several years on the road. If he travelled by land—and but few travellers in those days ever went from Constantinople to Rome by sea—his way would be through Thrace and Illyria, both just then teeming with religious excitement and episcopal gatherings; and if we credit him with having spent some time at a border-town of such celebrity as Aquileia, this is no more than S. Athanasius is known to have done in travelling from Rome to Sardica. Indeed it was at Aquileia, not Sardica, that the Council to which he was proceeding was to have met originally; and as at a council convened there by the Emperor Gratian thirty-five years afterwards, at which S. Ambrose was present, the only two remaining Arian bishops in those parts were deposed, its orthodoxy must have stood full as high then as its civic prestige. Marcellus, therefore, whether to learn Western manners or enlist the orthodox in his favour, is likely to have stopped at Aquileia longest of all places, if he travelled by land. At Aquileia, and possibly most places round it, he would find a creed in use which would have furnished him with the exact model on which that presented by him subsequently to Pope Julius as his own was framed, and which, we can hardly doubt, *must* : the Aquileian Creed, as I have transcribed it from the genuine Rufinus, being substantially word for word with his till just at its close: his closing with "The Resurrection of the body," *not* of this body, and "Life everlasting" in addition. Now, here it is precisely that the Eastern crops out. Easterns happened to be rather fond of ending their creeds just then as he has. "We believe," said the Council of Antioch,

A.D. 341, "in the Holy Ghost; and, if we should add anything else, we believe further in the resurrection of the body and life everlasting."* The Creed of Jerusalem, on which S. Cyril lectured A.D. 348,† the creed of the Eastern bishops who withdrew from the Council of Sardica the year before, had the same ending.‡ Even the longer of the two baptismal creeds published by S. Epiphanius as late as A.D. 373 had "Life everlasting" for its last article.§ As yet, indeed, this article was not in the Aquileian Creed, yet into this it was adopted first of any Western Creed—in the fifty years, namely,

---

* Soc. ii. 10.

† Heurtley, as before, p. 10.

‡ S. Hilar. Fragm. iii. § 29, and De Synod § 34, Ed. Migne. A note on the last of these passages shows that this formula was in reality that of the Council of Antioch, and had been sent into France by Narcissus and others as delegates from that Council to Constantinople, and was sent three years later into Italy by Eudoxius and others in an enlarged form.

§ Heurtley, p. 15.

that elapsed between Rufinus and S. Nicetas. S. Peter Chrysologus attests its presence in the Creed of Ravenna, whose communications with Aquileia must have been incessant, much about the same time; and from thence it passed westwards and to Rome. But it was above two hundred years more getting into general acceptance, as may be seen from the numerous specimens without it furnished by Professor Heurtley in his larger work.[*]

It is unnecessary to pursue the history of these additions in detail any further. One of them—"the descent into hell"—had been anticipated in a former chapter. And I have dwelt upon this particular one now less for its own sake than for the opportunity which it gave me of unravelling the origin of the Creed of Marcellus, and exhibiting it in its true colours. It was *not* the Roman; neither was it framed on the model of the Roman, but

[*] Harm. Symb. pp. 38-77, in which S. Augustine's different versions are included.

of the Western Creed: this Creed being also common to the African Church, and of the same family, but not by any means identical with the Roman, and at that time shorter, in reality, than the Creed of Marcellus by one Article.

By the end of the seventh century this creed had expanded to the exact form in most places which it has worn ever since. As it wanted a name, now that another creed was used in the Liturgy, it was called that of the Apostles; and as it had come to consist, or to be held to consist, of exactly twelve articles, it was ascribed to their joint composition. S. Isidore of Seville was, apparently, the first to credit the Apostles with its authorship, and to claim for it, as it stood then, a higher antiquity than for the Nicene. Pirminius, abbot in the diocese of Saragossa, led the way, about a century later,* in determining which Apostle composed

---

* Mabillon says A.D. 758. Migne's Patrol. lxxxix. 1030.

which article. These were fruitful themes for Charlemagne, who perceived their political value, and for those theologians who took their cue from him. Basilius of Ancyra had satisfied the Seventh Council of his orthodoxy, but there were two articles in the Western Creed—"Remission of sins" and "The resurrection of the body"—passed over in his profession. It is attacked by the author of the Caroline Books on both counts.* Of the first he says: "This article the Apostles are reported to have placed next to the confession of the Father, Son, and Holy Ghost in the compendium of faith, which they determined on before separating, as a rule of belief and preaching; and although studious of brevity there, to the extent described by the Prophet, where he says, 'A short word will the Lord make upon the earth:' still omit it they would not on any account, conscious that any profession without it would be neither

* iii. 6.

sincere nor complete." Of the second: "This also the Apostles included on all occasions among the other spiritual mysteries delivered by them when they went forth, endowed with different tongues, to instruct all nations and languages in the same faith." Gherbald, Bishop of Laon, is still more precise. "The Creed," he says, in bidding his clergy preach upon it conformably with instructions received from Charlemagne, "is what the Twelve Apostles arranged for our faith and belief in twelve versicles."* After such opinions had obtained generally, it is easy to see that it would have been strangely inconsistent with them to have gone on adding to the creed in question, little less than sacrilege to have enlarged it by a thirteenth article.

But there were two sets of canonical

---

* Mansi, xiii. 1084, and Charlemagne's letter, p. 1087. Comp. Leidrad, De Baptism. c. 4. Theodulph. De Ord. Bapt. c. 6. Eter. and Beat. Ep. ad Elipand. i. 87 and ii. 9, all in Migne's Patrol.

enactments overlapping or following each other about the same time, which contributed still more effectually to fix it to what it then was. The first of these relates to the learning of the Creed and Lord's Prayer by all as a devotional act, and may be given in the words of a canon attributed by Burchard and others to the Synod of Chalons on the Seine, A.D. 650. "It is to be ordered that the Lord's Prayer, in which all things necessary to the life of man are contained, and the Creed of the Apostles, in which the Catholic faith is contained in its integrity, be learnt by all, as well in Latin as in the vernacular, that what they profess with their mouths they may both understand and believe with their hearts." I begin with this instance to show the utter untrustworthiness of these collectors of canons in the dark ages. Anybody, who will be at the pains of referring to the two places in Mansi, will see that what Burchard ascribed to the Synod of

Chalons, forms, in reality, the second section of a capitulary by Haito, or Ahyto, Bishop of Basle, nearly two centuries later.* The earliest authentic enactments for teaching *everybody* this Creed and the Lord's Prayer combined that I can discover, date from the eighth century, and are few and far between before the reign of Charlemagne; however, there is one fact connected with their earlier history that should not be lost sight of: namely, that they commenced elsewhere than in Spain. Among the statutes of S. Boniface of Germany, A.D. 745,† we read, "Let the presbyters announce that all the faithful under their charge commit to memory the Creed and the Lord's Prayer: that by faith and prayer, the Holy Ghost assisting, they may obtain salvation." And again: "Let the presbyters announce that nobody, male or female, stand sponsor at

---

* Mansi, x. 1196, and xiv. 393.
† Mansi, xii. 385.

the holy font, who is unable to repeat the Creed and Lord's Prayer from memory." S. Cuthbert of Canterbury legislated similarly for the South of England a few years later; and the Synod of Calcuith, A.D. 785, on behalf of the North: "We have taught in our second chapter that all, without distinction, should know the Creed and the Lord's Prayer."

Charlemagne, when it came to his turn to enforce this, dogmatised as well as enacted: "First of all .... we propose that you note all those who can neither repeat from memory, nor are willing to learn the Lord's Prayer and Creed of the Christian faith: and that you cause them to come before us, and make them all, young and old, noble and ignoble, say, on coming thither, the Lord's Prayer and the Apostles' Creed, in which the fulness of the Catholic faith is contained; because, ' without faith '"—that is, from his point of view, *without dogma*—

"'it is impossible to please God.'"* He recurs to the same subject again and again in his other capitularies,† and in his letters to bishops, calling upon them to see that it was carried out by their clergy. Gherbald, Bishop of Laon, as will be remembered, was one of these; and the commencement of the pastoral issued by him in consequence, which has been in part anticipated, runs as follows: "First of all, we would admonish you, that we have long preached ourselves, and bade others preach on the Catholic faith and the Lord's Prayer..... The Lord's Prayer it is when we say, 'Our Father,' etc.; the Creed is what the twelve Apostles arranged for our faith and belief in twelve versicles." What he calls "the Catholic faith" in one place, he calls "the Apostles' Creed" in another; and this is precisely what I have quoted

---

* Mansi, xiii. 1090.
† Ib. 1093, and App. 171; also xiv. App. 256, 267, and 361.

him a second time to enable me to lay stress upon: namely, that throughout these capitularies "the Catholic faith" and "the Apostles' Creed" are apt to be regarded as synonymous terms, and used one for the other. A canonical epistle, printed among them by Mansi, says: "First of all let all presbyters, deacons, and sub-deacons commit to memory *the Catholic* faith."* .... One of the capitularies published at Aix-la-Chapelle, A.D. 789: "First of all we admonish that *the Catholic faith* be diligently read by all bishops and presbyters, and preached to all persons."† And the Forty-fifth Canon of the Synod of Mayence, A.D. 813: "Let the priests be constant in admonishing Christians to learn the Creed, which is the seal of faith, and the

* Mansi, xiii. 1095. The Ballerini (S. Leon. Op. iii. 955) claim a much earlier date for it, which they omit to prove; and explain the "Catholic faith" of the Athanasian Creed as though it *could mean* nothing else.

† Ib. App. 171.

Lord's Prayer." Presently, what they are required *to learn* is called "the Catholic faith."* The point of this observation will appear further on.

Thus, the Creed was no longer to be "delivered" to candidates for baptism exclusively: it was to enter into the devotions of all, be learnt by all, and constantly preached on in church to a promiscuous audience. Written copies of it would be rendered necessary, and speedily follow from its enlarged use. Nor was this all. A place for the Creed, in addition to the Lord's Prayer, before long suggested itself in the canonical hours, and became the subject of another set of enactments, which we need pursue no further than to their commencement.

In a Vatican MS. of the acts of the Synod of Aix-la-Chapelle, A.D. 816, there is, in addition to the long list of ecclesiastical ordinances common to all other copies of them, a sort of appendix

* Mansi, xiv. 73.

of supplemental regulations on most of the subjects previously dealt with, as though to reduce them to practice; but whether made then, or at another time or place, Mansi cannot decide.* Among these are directions for the saying of the second of the canonical, or first of the day hours, called "prime." And here provision is made for repeating the "Pater Noster," and the "Credo in Deum," in secret at the end of the lection, and after "Kyrie Eleison" thrice said.† The probability that this order was made then appears from hence. Amalarius, the well-known liturgical writer, and presbyter of Metz—a place likely to be uppermost in the minds of men for some time to come—is known to have drawn up his work, "Regula Canonicorum," at the instance of the Emperor Lewis, for approval by this Synod. This would naturally bring him into connection with its proceedings; and though his own

* xiv. 283.   † Ib. 305.

work, being entirely compiled from the Fathers and earlier councils, contained nothing to the purpose, there was another work, going by the same name, from which the Council culled largely, whose directions for saying the canonical hours were the most specific of any that had appeared hitherto, and which he of all others at Aix then must have known best: a "Regula Canonicorum," by Chrodegand, Bishop of Metz, about fifty years since. Now, in this work of Chrodegand there are directions for saying the Lord's Prayer at prime in the place and manner already described; but the Lord's Prayer only.* Yet Amalarius in another, and it would seem a subsequent work of his, in speaking of prime, testifies in express terms to the practice of saying the Creed, *as well as* the Lord's Prayer then,† just as if he had been commenting on these later directions. "*After the Lord's Prayer,*" he says, "follows our Belief which the

---

* C. 16. Patrol. xc. † De Eccl. Off. iv. 2.

Holy Apostles constructed, concerning the faith of the Holy Trinity, the dispensation of the Incarnation of our Lord, and the state of our Church."

As no such practice was in use when Chrodegand was Bishop of the same church only fifty years earlier, either the Church of Metz may have invented it in the interim and introduced it to this Council, or this Council invented it and introduced it to the Church of Metz. Of the two I rather incline to the former alternative; but in either case there can be no reason, so far as the use of the Creed is concerned, against supposing these directions to have emanated from this Synod of Aix, A.D. 816, whoever was the prompter of them. Either way, it was at this date that the Western Creed first began to be said at the canonical hours; and in the dominions of Charlemagne that this practice commenced and was enjoined. There is no mention of it whatever in the rule of S. Benedict, on which the Roman Office of those days was founded,* or, indeed, any other rules up to then :† and there is no hint, either in the works of Amalarius or in the canons of Aix-la-Chapelle, that it was then said at any other time than at the end of prime. The modern rubric, therefore, directing it to be said before matins and prime, and at the end of compline, was of course derived from hence, but is a much later arrangement. What is common to both is, that it was and is still directed to be said in secret when used.

* Palmer's Orig. Liturg. i. 213-16. Comp. Abbot Smaragdus on this rule, Patrol. cii. 829 *et seq.*

† *E.g.*, the anonymous rule in Mansi, xiv. 334, and Alcuin, "De Psalm. usu," and "Officia per Ferias." Patrol. cl. At p. 598 the original Nicene Creed occurs among prayers and hymns from various Fathers, but not as forming part of any service. The "Disput. Puer.," the "Lib. de Div. Off.," and "Symb. Expos.," which follow, are not his.

CHAPTER IV.

ON THE AGE, AIM, AND AUTHORSHIP OF THE ATHANASIAN CREED.

THERE is a third set of enactments, in addition to the two former already described, at one time running parallel to them, at another intermingling with them, that remains to be noticed; and noticed all the more carefully, as it brings us in sight of our proposed goal. Their subject is dogma.

Though they cannot well be separated into two classes, the earlier of these enactments have really two sides, and combine two distinct lines of thought: the first reared in Africa, then acclimatised in Spain, at length naturalised in all parts of the Latin Church; the second transplanted in maturity from the East, neglected or roughly handled on its introduction, and at length extinguished or lost in the other. Or, to put this in other words, they describe the rise and progress of theological dogma, so far as councils are concerned, in uncivilized and illiterate Europe.

The earliest specimen of the kind I mean is to be found in the first resolution of what is called the Second Council of Carthage, A.D. 390, where the presiding bishop says: * " To confirm the minds of our brethren and fellow-bishops lately promoted, let us propose that which, by certain tradition, we have received from the Fathers: that, as we have learnt the unity of the Trinity which we worship and adore—Father, Son, and Holy Ghost—to be without any diversity whatsoever, so we should teach it to the people of God." And all the bishops answered: "So we have received, so we

* Mansi, iii. 692.

hold unquestionably: following the faith of the Apostles." The heading of this canon or resolution is: "*Ut Trinitas credatur et predicetur.*"

Three years later a Synod of Hippo listened to S. Augustine, then a presbyter, "*disputing*," as he says himself, on this subject, and that of the Creed of his Church generally, in words that have been preserved, and now form one of the best known of his smaller works. "This Trinity," he told his hearers, "is one God: not that the Father is the same with the Son or with the Holy Ghost; but the Father being the Father, the Son the Son, and the Holy Ghost the Holy Ghost, this Trinity is one God, as it is written: 'Hear, O Israel, the Lord thy God is one God.' At the same time, should we be asked of each in this way: 'Is the Father God?' we reply, 'He is God;' 'Is the Son God?' we reply, 'Yes;' and of the Holy Ghost just the same. Not by any means as it is said

in the psalms of men: 'Ye are Gods.'"*
In this work S. Augustine refers more than once to the "learned and spiritual men" who had written on the Trinity before him, but he nowhere cites them as authorities whom he must follow implicitly; on the contrary, because none of them had† " disputed hitherto with sufficient fulness and perspicuity respecting the Holy Ghost," as he says, he is all the more copious in speculating upon this article himself, and is soon in advance of the boldest till then. It is superfluous to say that the Niceno-Constantinopolitan Creed, though it had been published twelve years, is nowhere named in his work. It was never received at all in Africa that I can discover. As yet there had been no formal acceptance by the African Church, even of the Creed of Nicæa. This Creed was formally received there, for the first time, at what is called

* " De Fide et Symb." § 16.
† Ibid. § 19.

the eighteenth of the Councils of Carthage, under Aurelian, A.D. 419, when it was incorporated into the African code; but by then everybody that had a turn for theological inquiries in Africa was shaping his views from the larger work on the Trinity of the great Bishop of Hippo, which, according to his own statement, excited so much interest there long before it came out that the first twelve books of it were stolen from him and circulated in an unfinished state.* Yet this work is but a matured and highly-finished expression of the other. Later writers in Africa who discoursed on the Trinity, finding they could add nothing to his speculations, only thought of putting his conclusions into dogmatic shape, and enunciating them with an air of positiveness from which he recoiled himself.

---

* Retract. ii. 15. From the dedicatory letter to Bishop Aurelian it appears that he was prevented correcting them as much as he could have wished in consequence.

To the same influences, unquestionably, must be ascribed "the rule of faith" said to have been drawn up in Spain long before the introduction of the Niceno-Constantinopolitan Creed, at the Third Council of Toledo, by King Reccared, A.D. 589, and it was in the spirit of this rule that even he dogmatised in his opening address, afterwards interpolating the Creed, as if to make both square. It shall be given in the shape in which it stands in the collections of Councils as a sample, not by any means that this was its original shape:*

> We believe in one God, the Father, Son, and Holy Ghost, Maker of things visible and invisible, by Whom all things were created in heaven and in earth. That this one God and this one Trinity belong to the Divine Essence. That the Father, however, is not the Son, but has a Son Who is not the Father. That the Son is not the Father, but is the Son of God, of the nature of the Father;

---

* See comments of Pagi, given in Mansi, iii. 1001; and my own remarks, "Christendom's Divisions," ii. 431.

that the Holy Ghost, also, is one Who is neither the Father nor the Son, but proceeds from the Father and the Son. So the Father is unbegotten, and the Son unbegotten, and the Holy Ghost not begotten, but proceeding from the Father and the Son. It is the Father Whose voice was heard from heaven, saying: "This is my Son, in Whom I am well pleased;" the Son, Who says: "I went forth from the Father, and came from God into this world;" the Holy Ghost, of Whom the Son says: "Unless I go away to the Father, the Paraclete will not come to you." That this Trinity, distinguished by persons, united in substance, is in might, power, and majesty both indivisible and without diversity; neither, besides It, is there any divine nature, whether of angel, spirit, or power whatsoever, which we believe, or which any should believe to be God. That this Son of God, accordingly, God born of the Father prior to any beginning whatsoever, sanctified the womb of the Virgin Mary, and, without any carnal generation, assumed true man of her: two natures alone, the Godhead and the flesh, combining in one sole Person, our Lord Jesus Christ, in Whom there was neither an imaginary, nor in any sense phantastic body, but a true and solid one. That He hungered and thirsted, grieved and wept, and endured all bodily pains. That He was crucified by the Jews, buried, and rose the third day; conversed afterwards with His disciples, and ascended, the fortieth day after His resurrection, into heaven. That this Son of Man is also called the Son of

God: and we call the Lord, the Son of God, the Son of Man. We believe there will be a resurrection of the human flesh; and as for the soul of man, we call it neither a divine substance, nor equal with God, but a creature created by the Divine will.

The only thing oriental about this "rule" is its commencement: "We believe in one God;" but the Africans themselves, after the Nicene Creed had been received amongst them, got into the habit of commencing their professions in the same manner, as we have seen already; and its own African caste is disclosed in the same parapraph by making the universe created, not by the Father, as in the Western Creed, nor by the Father and the Son, as in the Niceno-Constantinopolitan Creed, but by the whole Trinity, which was S. Augustine's pet dogma. And it is African all through, with one exception—the paragraph, namely, declaring the whole work of the Incarnation to have been the act of the Son alone, without any reference to the Holy

Ghost, which was, doubtless, original. There were sixteen Councils of Toledo, beginning with the third, at which the Niceno-Constantinopolitan Creed was received, and following each other for rather more than a century, where, if there was any dogmatism at all, it was of a piece with this rule, whatever its length, in being either African or Gothic. The form it takes is either that of a prefatory discourse from the King, of which there are several characteristic specimens, or else that of a canon or capitulary, headed "De evidenti Catholicæ fidei veritate," as at the Fourth Council; or "De plenitudine fidei Catholicæ," as at the Sixth. Where there is any dogmatism, the creed is seldom recited; and whether recited or not, it is never really commented upon. On one occasion* the President, King Recevinth, apologised naïvely for this omission by saying: "This holy rule of faith is, therefore, given on this occasion

* Viz. the Eighth Council. Mansi, x. 1206.

without comment, because it has been expounded abundantly by holy doctors ere now, *and business of urgent moment imposes upon us other occupations.*" In every case where the creed is recited, it is with the interpolated clause due to King Reccared: and if six Councils out of the sixteen profess their agreement with the first four General Councils, it is with the first four only. Then, at the fifteenth or last of these, King Egica, while professing his adhesion to the first four General Councils, argues vehemently for several dogmatic positions against Pope Benedict II., who had disapproved of them."*

I have given prominence to these facts to illustrate the bold line taken by these pioneers of Western dogmatism, whenever their own speculations were trenched upon. They pledged themselves to the

---

* Mansi, tom. xii., 10. Comp. the Dogmatic Statement of the Sixteenth Council. Mansi, x. p. 64.

faith of the first four councils, but interpolated the creed ordained by the fourth; they took no more notice of the Fifth Council than if no such council had met, though they could not have been ignorant that its rejection was causing a schism elsewhere; and if, again, they attest having had the acts of the Sixth Council sent them for acceptance by the Pope, after declaring, they will accept it so far as it accords with the first four, they proceed to dogmatise themselves upon the points defined by it in their own fashion.* And on the next Pope finding fault with their theology, they reiterate their positions in his teeth, bidding the world take note that he is wrong and they right.

But the chief singularity by far of all their proceedings is, that while they dogmatise with S. Augustine, they never so much as name the Creed of his Church, which was that of the West also.† The

* Caps. 6 and 8-10. Mansi, xi., 1089-90.
† Can. 1 of the Third Council of Braga, A.D.

only creed they ever profess is that of the Fourth Council, formally received, indeed, by them "according to the form of the Eastern Churches," but accommodated in reality to their own views. Their teaching, again, was confessedly that of the African Church; but what they say of it themselves is that it is all in harmony with the faith of the first four councils, the only councils to which they ever appeal.

Consequently, when we come to estimate their effect upon European theology, so much greater than is in general supposed, we must distinguish accurately between their dogmatism and their creed. Their dogmatism and their creed not having been connected originally, so far as either had any distinctive character, they were not inseparable, except of course to the extent that one had been received

572, orders that catechumens should be taught the "Credo in Deum;" etc., but this was before the conversion of King Reccared, and it is possible that "unum" may have slipped out even here before "Deum."

into the other. Accordingly, the one link that bound them together was the "*Filioque*" clause in the creed. They were so far correlative, and no further. On the other hand, all other Western nations had a creed of their own, substantially word for word with the African Creed, and were by no means unacquainted with African theology, which had in earlier times penetrated into the South of France by another route: viz., by way of Lerins and Marseilles.

These remarks may serve to explain what actually took place. The Third of the Councils of Toledo met A.D. 589, and the eighteenth, or last of them, A.D. 701. Their influence would begin about the same time, subsequently to the former, that it would survive the latter. Thus, A.D. 650, we find traces of it as far north as Chalons on the Seine, where a canon was then passed in these words:

"We have defined unanimously and with one accord, that the rule of faith, as piously professed at the Nicene Council, handed down by the holy Fathers, and explained by them, or as it was afterwards confirmed by the holy Council of Chalcedon, be maintained in all things and by all."*

And at Braga, to the north of Oporto, where the Western Creed had apparently been taught, A.D. 572, the first canon of a council held there rather more than one hundred years later, speaks of the Niceno-Constantinopolitan Creed, which it recites with the interpolation of King Reccared, as "our own rule of faith."†
It had been called "our belief" by a Synod of Merida nine years before.‡ And it was doubtless intended to be paraphrased five years later by our own forefathers at the Synod of Hatfield in these words:

* Mansi, x. 1190.
† Ib. xi., 153. And for the previous Synod, ix. 838.
‡ Ib. xi. 77.

"We have set forth the right and orthodox faith, as delivered by our Lord Jesus Christ to his Apostles, and handed down in the creed of the holy Fathers ... confessing the Father, Son, and Holy Spirit: the Holy Trinity in Unity, and the Unity in Trinity: one God in Three consubstantial Persons of equal honour and glory. . . . God the Father, without beginning; His Only-begotten Son, born of the Father before all worlds; and the Holy Spirit, proceeding ineffably from the Father and the Son, according to the preaching of the above-named Apostles, and prophets, and doctors: to all which we have subscribed, who with Archbishop Theodore have expounded the Catholic faith."

Archbishop Theodore, who presided at Hatfield, was a Greek; but Abbot Adrian, his inseparable "assistant," by whom Pope Vitalian* had expressly pro-

---

* See my Historical Tract on the "*Filioque*" clause, p. 18-19. Rivingtons, 1867.

vided that his proceedings should be closely watched, was a learned African. The fact of his presence would go far to account for the dogmatic turn of this paraphrase; but in that it affects to have been drawn from the Creed, we must infer, also, that the interpolated creed had by then been received in England.

Two more professions of the Nicene faith remain to be noticed: one pure and simple, the other in connection with the faith of the six first general councils. The first is a capitulary, published at Soissons apparently by King Pepin: "That the Catholic faith settled by the three hundred and eighteen bishops forming the Nicene Council should be preached throughout our whole realm."* The second emanated from the Synod of Calcuith in Northumberland, A.D. 787, which commenced its capitularies by ordaining that "the holy and inviolate faith of the Nicene Council should be

* Mansi, xii. App. iii.

maintained faithfully and firmly by all who are destined for the service of the sanctuary; and that in synodical meetings every year the presbyters of each church, whose duty it was to instruct the people, should be themselves examined diligently respecting the faith in general, so that they may in all things confess, maintain, and preach the Apostolical and universal faith of the six councils, approved by the Holy Ghost, as it has been delivered to us by the holy Roman Church; and may not fear to die for it, should opportunity offer; receiving whomsoever those holy general councils received, and condemning and rejecting from the heart everybody that they condemned."*

From this date references to the Nicene faith cease. It is far otherwise with the dogmatism of the Councils of Toledo, and with their creed. Of their creed all that need be said is that it is in use still all over the West, just as King Reccared

* Mansi, xii. 937.

published it; and not more inaccurately named than the Creeds of the Apostles and S. Athanasius.

On their dogmatism a few words more must be added. The form it took, as I have stated already, was that of a prefatory discourse, canon, or capitulary, sometimes emanating from the monarch who convened them, sometimes from the bishops, or presiding bishop, present, but always on one theme; and this for the most part expressed in its title: viz. "on the Catholic faith." Of course, so far as the "Catholic faith" and the "Creed" were synonymes — and it occasionally named them as such—so far it treated of both alike; but in its hands the "Catholic faith" in reality covered a much wider range, and it never professedly took the "Creed" for its text. It affected, if it nowhere professed, to be supplemental to the creed. If it limited itself to topics expressed in the creed, it resolved questions respecting them on which the

OF THE ATHANASIAN CREED. 207

creed is silent, and drew inferences from them which wore the appearance, to say the least, of new truths. Its tone was that of self-assurance and menace; and what it particularly luxuriated in was the systematic employment of terms from which the framers of the creed, and in some cases even the founder of itself had pointedly shrank. By the founder of itself, I mean S. Augustine; and by the creed, the Niceno-Constantinopolitan— for to this it was attached in Spain— at the head of whose framers I place S. Athanasius.*

S. Athanasius justified the introduction of one word that was unscriptural into the creed, and of but one: "We are not baptized in the name of the *Unbegotten*, nor do we address ourselves to the *Unbegotten* in the Lord's Prayer:"† he

* For reasons that will appear in Dr. Smith's forthcoming Dict. of Christ. Antiq. Art. "Councils of Constantinople."

† De Dec. Synod. Nic. c. 31. Op. i. 236. Ed. Ben.

says, even in defending the Nicene decrees. Whether he would have sanctioned the word "Trinity," or not, in any more private formula, we may not be perhaps able to say; but its absence, and the absence of any such terms,* in asserting doctrine, from his own authentic "Exposition of the Faith," is at least noteworthy, coupled with one of the gravest of his public acts. At the end of his long and glorious career, after his own judgment had been ripened by experience, after his name had become a proverb in all lands for orthodoxy, and all eyes were fixed on the council assembled by him, A.D. 362, on returning from exile to give peace to Christendom, application having been made to it by two contending parties to decide whether the "Hypostasis" of the Father, Son, and Holy

* The word "hypostasis" occurs once, and but once: and then as a disclaimer—"To imagine three hypostases," he says, "divided from each other, as men are by their bodies, would be to fall into Polytheism."

OF THE ATHANASIAN CREED. 209

Ghost was to be considered distinct or the same—in other words, whether the term "Hypostasis" meant "Person" or "Substance"—the council, acting doubtless under his inspiration, deprecated using any such expressions at all in speaking of God;* and still more fixing their meaning too rigidly. Further: "Should any propose to add explanations to the Creed of Niceæ"—such was its advice to the East and West alike—"silence all such, and persuade them rather to study to be peaceable; for such conduct in our opinion can only spring from a love of controversy and nothing else."†

It was due to this excellent counsel that the Niceno-Constantinopolitan Creed is recited in the East to this day, word for word, as it was promulgated by the Fourth Council; nay, more, that whatever the heresies condemned there

* Ὀυκ ἐπὶ Θεοῦ δεῖν ἔφασαν, ταύταις χρῆσθαι ταῖς λέξεσι. Soc. iii. 6.
† Mansi, iii. 348-49.

since the days of S. Athanasius, "Homoousios" is still its single exception to the Scriptural language in which it is couched.

Strange phenomenon, that Eastern and Western Africa, separated merely by the desert of sand that borders on each alike, should have produced theological schools diverging so widely, to say nothing of their other peculiarities,* as those represented by SS. Athanasius and Augustine; at the same time, as S. Augustine cannot consistently with history be said to have created those influences which he above all others rendered attractive, so neither would it be fair to credit him with the often reckless and always more pronounced tone of his followers.

On the point in question, for instance,

* "Christendom's Divisions," i. 66 : " Egypt, or Eastern Africa, in S. Athanasius, laid down unerringly the science of what may be called Christian divinity: Algeria, or Western Africa, in the person of S. Augustine, laid down unerringly the science of what may be called Christian humanity for the universal Church of all ages and lands."

the using of unscriptural terms, Tertullian had in his work against Praxeas, almost two centuries earlier, used both the word "person," and "trinity" in describing the Godhead; and in his own time the Second Council of Carthage directed, as we have seen, all to teach the Trinity in Unity as they had received it from the Fathers. Not having as yet received the Nicene Creed themselves, the African bishops could not well have been thinking of the Fathers who framed it when they said this; at all events with our existing materials we may well doubt those words having come from those Fathers, though their teaching would of course imply them: those words not having found their way into *Greek theology** till after the Nicene Council.

* I mean this *strictly*; for Tertullian wrote some works in Greek, as he tells us himself: and in the work of S. Dionysius of Rome against Sabellius, which so far as it has been preserved, is in Greek also, the phrase "Divine Triad" occurs more than once. From these fragments being in

At the same time, it is also certain that nothing had passed at the Nicene, or any other council, to prevent those words, "unity" and "trinity" being used ever so freely. And having been employed thus freely by a Council of Carthage, for S. Augustine to have shown any misgivings in using them afterwards would have been strange indeed. But S. Augustine may have heard also somewhat of the rulings of the Council of Alexandria —whether from S. Ambrose, at whose feet he once sat, and into whose immemediate neighbourhood they must have been carried by Eusebius of Vercelli, the energetic assistant of S. Athanasius in framing them, or else from his own

Greek, this Pope has been supposed a Greek by birth; but the question is, are these fragments preserved solely by being cited in SS. Athanasius and Basil, his "ipsissima verba," or their translations from the Latin? The work of the Roman presbyter, Novatian, his contemporary, which is in Latin, and has been *entitled* "De Trinitate," contains no such word. For both see Migne's Patrol. iii. 885; and v. 109-16.

Bishop Valerian, who was a Greek—on the word "Hypostasis:" and this most probably dictated his own reserve about the word "person," its Latin equivalent.

In his earlier works intended for popular instruction we seem to miss it altogether. It either never occurs at all in his "Euchiridon," for instance: or his four books on "Christian Doctrine," or his "Sermon to Catechumens on the Creed," or his treatises "On Faith and the Creed," on "Faith and Works," and on "The Faith of Things not Seen;" or else not where he is engaged on the Trinity. In the 39th of his Tractates on S. John,* nothing that his supposed adversary can say will induce him to pronounce the word. "Three what, you ask? I reply, Father, Son, and Holy Ghost. Count yourself. Have not I named three? That which the Father is in relation to Himself is God; that which He is in relation to the Son is

* § 3. He is commenting on c. viii. 26-7.

the Father, and so forth. Thus God is neither removed from number nor comprehended by number. Because there are three, there is as it were number: but ask, three what? and directly there is no number."

Overcome by the "necessities of the case," such is his own account of it in his work on the Trinity, he resigns himself at last, hopeless of devising anything better, to a terminology, which others before him entitled to his respect had used. " One essence or substance, but three persons;" as many Latins, worthy to be considered authorities, in treating of this subject have said, unable to discover any more suitable manner of expressing in words what they realized in their minds without words... Still they said *Three persons*, not because they desired it said, but rather than remain silent when asked.*" Even then he was

---

* v. 9. So vii. 4: "Placuit ita dici, ut diceretur aliquid cum quæreretur quid tria sunt, quæ

only treading in the beautiful course, which he had traced for himself at starting. Whenever I hesitate, I shall never be ashamed of inquiring; nor of learning, whenever I am wrong... Let me beg of my readers to go with me, when equally certain; inquire with me when they hesitate to the same extent; come back to me when they find themselves, call me back to them when they find *me* wrong."* How sublimely superior in all this to the arrogant hard lines of his followers!

Those sixteen Councils of Toledo, contrariwise, judging from their general tone, would have visited any with the same penalties for objecting to call the Father, Son, and Holy Ghost persons, as for refusing to confess each and all of them God. But I must not anticipate what

---

tria esse fides vera pronuntiat . . . Quid igitur restat, nisi ut fatemur loquendi necessitate parta hæc vocabula." . . .

* i. 3.

I shall have to say on the intrinsic character of their rulings hereafter; as yet we have by no means done with the form which they assumed.

I have said that the title borne by one of their capitularies is, " On the fulness of the Catholic Faith." This capitulary neither contains nor appeals to the creed in any way. But the heading of another is the same, where the creed alone had been recited, and the King apologised for leaving it without comment. On another occasion, viz. at the Seventeenth Council, it was recited after some prefatory remarks, ending thus: " With our mouths we make profession of the articles of the creed, which contains the sacrament of the whole of our holy faith." Charlemagne, we may remember, applied this identical language to the Western Creed: " Symbolum Apostolorum, ubi Catholicæ fidei plenitudo continetur." We now see where he borrowed it. Nor is this all. The " Catholic faith" and the Western or "Apostles' Creed" constantly go together in his capitularies, but *never* the "Catholic faith" and the Niceno-Constantinopolitan Creed, as in Spain. With this single exception, he and his bishops made these Councils of Toledo their dogmatic model. At the Council of Frankfort, that is, by comparison, in his younger days, he had the assurance to attack the Second Nicene Council for having departed from what he asserted to have been the faith of the First; but Pope Adrian having utterly demolished this illusion in his bold rejoinder to the Caroline Books, their royal author, as if to conceal his defeat, abstained in the most marked manner himself, and, doubtless, influenced others to abstain equally, from ever appealing again to the Nicene faith. The Council of Calcuith, in England, as I have stated, was the last to do so for many a long day. Nobody can fail to be struck with this coincidence.* Fortu-

* I have gone through vols. xiii. and xiv. of

nately for him, there was a creed indigenous in his own dominions, for which far higher antiquity, far more distinguished authorship had been claimed. And to this he appeals to his capitularies, and to this only. If it was somewhat too simple for his turn of mind, he could follow the precedent of the Toledo Fathers, and supplement it by dogmatism like theirs. He might copy their manner throughout;

Mansi, containing all Councils and Capitularies to the middle of the ninth century, without finding one such. Charlemagne's 31st Capitulary of one year, Mansi thinks A.D. 789, which is headed "De fide Trinitatis prædicanda," cites the African Canon already quoted, and appends the original Creed of Nicæa, just as it is appended to the African code, but with this rather amusing difference—that of its origin no more is said here than this: "A *Magno Synodo* dictum est;" and a date is given to it which seems intended to mystify. Append. to vol. xii. p. 164. Append. to vol. xiv. p. 267, contains a Capitulary of A.D. 802, headed "Admonitio de Symbolo fidei," which is probably his own summary of what all should believe. Most of the Councils of this period had a canon headed "De fide Catholicà;" but none of these refer in any way to the Nicene faith.

he might at times apply the same name to both: at one time what he would mean by the "Catholic faith" should be his or their exposition of the Catholic faith; at another the creed, not of Nicæa or Constantinople, but of the Apostles themselves, with which it would be found in strict accord. Hence the repetition of ambiguities already noticed in his capitularies. Presbyters are told to learn the "Catholic faith" by heart, which, of course, there means "the Creed. Bishops and presbyters, to preach the "Catholic faith," which is sometimes called the "Creed" in the next sentence, sometimes *may* mean more, and sometimes *must*. It must mean more, naturally, where the Creed is specified in addition, as at Frankfort, for instance: "That the Catholic faith of the Holy Trinity, the Lord's Prayer, and the symbol of faith be preached and delivered to all. Here we have plainly three things specified, not two—the first to be "preached," and the last two "delivered." What is called "the Catholic faith of the Holy Trinity" at starting is anything but mere tautology for what is afterwards called the "symbol of faith" or creed. Waterland conjectured that by the former must have been meant the Athanasian Creed, but he was mistaken. As yet the " Catholic faith" meant only the dogmatic expositions of it in general then in vogue—nothing, literally, more specific than what the Second Council of Carthage had enjoined on this head. There had long been a craving, to be sure, for something more specific, and this had been so often attempted without any real success as to have become, more or less, a positive need. *Whose* epitome of the Catholic faith, as distinct from the Creed, should be followed? Should it be that of the Third Council of Toledo, framed by King Reccared, or of the fourth, which was that of S. Isidore? of the eleventh, which was that of a bishop again? or of the sixteenth, which was that of another king? Again and again Charlemagne referred to his prelates and wise men for some standard formula, and they both agreed with him, and amongst themselves, in making S. Paul say that "without faith"—*i.e.* without faith cast into proper dogmatic mould—"it was impossible to please God." Several had tried their hands—Alcuin,* by his own confession, among the number, several times,† to no purpose; but at last one succeeded. As he is not so well known as he used to be, he should not, perhaps, be brought under notice without some slight introduction. Aquileia was, as I

---

* See, for instance, Alcuin's first words: De Trin. i., 1.

† Ep. cx. (Ed. Migne), "In libello . . . quem direximus . . . vobis solatium et confirmationem fidei Catholicæ. Sed in manibus majus modo habemus opus." . . . Another was styled his "Confessio fidei," (Patrol. ci. 1003.) Another was "On the Catholic Faith," composed at the instance of Archbishop Arno. (Ep. clxi.) The best known was his work "On the Faith of the Holy Trinity," dedicated to Charlemagne.

stated in connection with Rufinus a long way back, the only Western See that boasted of a Patriarch besides Rome: and from the days of Augustus it had, of all other cities in Italy, ranked next to Rome. It stood, consequently, to Rome, when compared with other cities of Italy, *much as Alexandria stood to Rome* when compared with other cities of the world. Thus it might claim to be literally, both in Church and State, *the Alexandria of Italy*. And if its walls and palaces had been twice ruined by the Huns and Lombards, it attained to greater ecclesiastical splendour than it had ever enjoyed before under Charlemagne and his descendants. Of this see the first prelate who had caused himself to be styled Patriarch was named Paulinus. Another of the same name and dignity, but incomparably more famed for his attainments, and venerated all the world over for his years and strikingly grave deportment, occupied it at the close of the eighth century. He may be said, without exaggeration, to have been idolised by such men as Alcuin, and even inspired Charlemagne with awe. He was the episcopal soul of the Council of Frankfort, and president as well as soul of that of Friuli, both of which have left their mark upon history. When he had written against Felix, Bishop of Urgel, in Spain, and founder of the sect called Adoptionists, he was thought to have exhausted the controversy. "Aquileia locuta, causa finita est." Such was the tone of his admirers. "Should you have occasion to see Patriarch Paulinus," says Alcuin, writing to Arno, Archbishop of Saltzburg, "salute him a thousand thousand times. I have just finished reading his book of the Catholic faith, which he sent to the lord King, and so pleased was I with its eloquence and flowers of speech, its handling of the faith and its weight of authorities, that I think any further discussion of the topics at issue between ourselves and the partisans of Felix superfluous. And happy is the Church and People of Christ as long as, besides the lord King, it shall possess but one such defender of the Catholic faith." . . . . . . There was more to be done still, it was true, but error had been confuted once for all in this treatise."*

The letter in which this passage occurs appears as edited by Migne in a much longer, and in his opinion a more complete form than it had when first published; there would be little difficulty, nevertheless, in proving the bracketed portions of it to be detached fragments— all indeed written by Alcuin, but neither at one time nor to one person—by some transcriber afterwards combined in one. There can be no doubt, for instance, that Alcuin is here referring to the work of Paulinus against Felix, in three books, dedicated to Charlemagne; and this work,

Ep. 108, Ed. Migne. Alcuin's works are in vols. c. and ci. of his Patrol.

according to the elaborate showing of Madrisius, appeared A.D. 796, the year in which the Council of Friuli met under his presidency.* Alcuin, plainly, could not have left a work of that importance long unnoticed; and even his acknowledgment that Adoptionism had survived it, points to the same conclusion.

Four years after the work against Felix had appeared, we find Alcuin writing again—A.D. 800, according to Migne †—and this time to Paulinus himself, in a state of mind bordering upon ecstasy, created by the recent perusal of a work of his, yet expressed in anything but unmeaning platitudes. Inflated as was the style of those days, few people could, I think, read what is there said of it, without feeling curious to identify the work, of which so famous a scholar and theologian as Alcuin could so write;

* Diss. iv. Hist. Crit. in Migne's Patrol. xcix. 545-92. Also "The Life," c. 7.
† Ep. cxiii.

and when each of the acknowledged works of Paulinus that have come down to us had been gauged successively by this praise of his friend, still fewer would probably dissent from the conclusion of its latest expositor: "All this, in my opinion, must refer to some work of Paulinus that has not yet seen daylight;"* or, what *may prove to be the same thing*, to some work that has not yet been acknowledged as his. Let us see whether Alcuin has not in reality named the *only possible work* by describing it as he has. I shall extract enough from his letter to enable my readers to decide this point for themselves:

"To my most beloved lord in the Lord of lords, and holy father, Patriarch Paulinus, greeting:

"I seem to have been refreshed inwardly, that the hidden flame of charity within my heart may be able to elicit at least some spark, lest that be extinguished

* Annot. ad l. ed. Migne.

which burns within me, now that I have opportunity to write something to one so dear. What! when I have the privilege of looking upon letters from you sweeter than honey, do I not seem to hold converse wholly with all the flowers of Paradise, and with the eager hand of desire to pluck from thence spiritual fruits? how much more, then, on perusing *the tract* ('libellum') *of your most holy faith,* adorned with all the *spotlessness of Catholic peace; eloquent and attractive in style to the highest degree; in the truth of its ideas firm as a rock* .... where, as from one bright and salutary fountain in Paradise, I beheld the streams of the four virtues irrigating not merely the rich plains of Italy, but *the entire demesne of ecclesiastical Latinity.* Where, too, *I beheld the golden outpourings of spiritual ideas commingling abundantly with the gems of scholastic polish.* Certainly you have achieved a work of immense profit and prime necessity *in appraising the Catholic faith as you have:*[*] the very thing I have so long desired myself, and so often urged upon the King, to get a symbol of the Catholic faith, plain in meaning and lucid in phrase, reduced to one compendious form, and given to all priests in each parish of every diocese to read, and commit to memory, so that

---

[*] " Quam plurimis vero profuturum et pernecessarium fecistis opus in Catholicæ fidei *taxatione*," etc. The exact meaning of this word in Alcuin's mouth, is seen illustrated in the terse, dogmatic summary given by the author of the Caroline Books himself, and ending thus: " Hæc est Catholicæ traditionis fidei vera integritas, quam sincero corde credimus et fatemur: et in hoc opere, beati Hieronymi verbis expressam, *taxavimus*." Whether I have rendered it by the best English equivalent is another question.

everywhere the same faith might be heard uttered by a multitude of tongues. Lo! what I had desired in my humility, has been supplied by your genius. With the Author of our salvation you have earned for yourself a perpetual reward of this good intention, and *praise amongst men for this perfect work.*"

Like the former one, this letter ends with a reference to Spain, but in marked contrast connects it with Adoptionism no longer. That cloud had disappeared wholly from the horizon, and, with the exception of a slight haziness in the administration of baptism in some quarters, and on the intermediate state between death and judgment in others, all was bright and at rest there. This letter, accordingly, cannot have been written till Adoptionism had been extinguished; in other words before A.D. 800, which was the year in which Charlemagne was crowned emperor. I have printed in italics those parts of it which I consider highly specific, and in large type what I consider absolutely distinctive. Most people will agree with me that one set of expressions is singularly descriptive of the Athanasian Creed: I hope to prove to their satisfaction that the other can describe nothing else. Most people will, again, be disposed to grant at starting that, had the Athanasian Creed been in existence previously, either Alcuin could not have known of it, or else must have been singularly forgetful of it, or blind to its excellence to have written thus; and yet he cites it himself solemnly two or three years later, as we shall see. So far as regards its having "received perpetual praise amongst men as a perfect work," or its combination of "spiritual ideas with scholastic polish," its "irrigating the entire domain of ecclesiastical Latinity," in other words, the whole Latin Church, the " adamantine strength of its verities," and the " eloquence and attractiveness of its style," Alcuin may deserve to be called alternately a critic of discernment or a true prophet. But in that he has described *Paulinus* as "*having supplied*" the very desideratum of which he himself had been so long in quest: a symbol of the Catholic faith, plain in meaning and lucid in phrase, reduced to one compendious form, to be given to all priests to commit to memory, so that everywhere the same faith might be heard uttered by a multitude of tongues, he has solved a long-vexed historical problem for us of high interest, which, but for this stray letter of his, might never have been unlocked to the end of time, but which, touched with the key supplied here, tells its own tale, from beginning to end, in the simplest form.

To introduce the reader to this at once,

without further preliminaries, I must ask him to take my word here for what I shall hope to authenticate for him by facts hereafter, though Alcuin may have convinced him of it already: that up to this time there are no testimonies to the existence of the so-called Athanasian Creed that will bear criticism for a moment extant; that from this very year they are both numerous and continuous; and that for some time from this year also they divide themselves into two classes, apparently distinct, but fraught with evidence of the same intention. I shall confine myself in this chapter to such testimonies as are indisputable, and, as I stated, date from this year, considering, however, but one class first, viz. that for which Alcuin was, doubtless, responsible. A.D. 800, then, at the earliest, Alcuin compliments Paulinus enthusiastically on having "supplied a symbol of the Catholic faith" precisely of the kind he wanted, and had repeatedly spoken about to Charlemagne, for priests to learn by heart. Two years from this, at the latest, or A.D. 802, a Synod met at Aix, under Charlemagne, at which Alcuin's own work "On the Faith of the Holy Trinity" was read and approved, at which Paulinus himself seems to have been a leading personage,* and at which a "General Capitulary" was passed, containing, amongst other things, provisions "for the instruction of the clergy," which commence thus:

"These are the things which all ecclesiastics are commanded to learn:

1. "The Catholic faith of S. Athanasius, and all other things on the faith.

2. "The Apostles' Creed also.

3. "The Lord's Prayer to be understood thoroughly with its exposition."

And other items.†

Alcuin and Paulinus both died, A.D.

* Madrisius says "as legate of the Pope," but this sounds mythical. See Migne's Patrol. xcix., Life, c. 2.

† Pertz, Monum. Germ. Legum, i. 105-9.

804, so that this was almost their last work; but it survived them. The capitularies of Theodulph, Bishop of Orleans, their junior by some years, contain a similar ordinance:

"Wherefore, we admonish you, O priests of the Lord, that you both retain in your memory, and understand with your hearts, the Catholic faith: that is, the 'I believe,' and 'Whosoever will be saved, before all things it is necessary that he hold the Catholic faith.'"*

In another work of his, to be quoted presently, Theodulph calls the latter expressly, " the Creed of S. Athanasius." Shortly afterwards—and of course with the same object of getting it learnt by heart—it was ordered to be recited, like the Apostles' Creed, at prime. Among the directions for saying the day-hours attributed to the Synod of Aix, A.D. 816, on which some remarks have been made previously, we read: "On Saturday, the

* Cap. 2. Mansi, xiii. 1009.

Psalms 'Confitemini Domino' and 'Deus in Nomine,' as above: to which on the Lord's Day* let the 'Catholic faith' be added, which is to be sung with heart and voice, and by nobody with the head covered. Afterwards the lection, then the 'Kyrie Eleison' thrice repeated, followed by the 'Pater Noster' and 'Credo,' said privately." I quote the whole to show that by the "Catholic faith" is *here* meant something distinct from the Creed. But, again, what is meant by the "Catholic faith" in this passage, is at once seen from the following injunction of Haito or Ahyto, Bishop of Basle, some years later.

"Fourthly, that the faith of S. Athanasius be learnt by priests, and recited from the heart on the Lord's Day at prime."†

Later by thirty years Hincmar, the well-known Archbishop of Rheims, or-

---

* Mansi, xiv. 305, where the reading (posssibly, a misprint) is "omni die."

† Mansi, 395.

dained: "That every priest should fully learn the exposition of the Creed and of the Lord's Prayer, according to the tradition of the orthodox Fathers ... and also commit to memory the discourse of Athanasius on the faith, beginning with 'Whosoever will be saved:' so as to understand it thoroughly, and be able to put it into plain language."* About the same time, the injunctions of Bishop Haito were republished *verbatim* by the Emperor Lewis II.†

Obviously enough, a practice like this would require time to spread in those disorganised ages; and amidst the fierce broils that ensued between the grandsons of Charlemagne particularly, we cannot be surprised that a formula become habitual in one kingdom or diocese, should seem long afterwards all but unknown in another.‡ However, in process

---

* Mansi, xv. 475.
† Pertz, Monum. Germ. Legum, i. 439.
‡ Even during the life-time of Charlemagne

of time, what Alcuin had advised became law for all; and to this day the Athanasian Creed is committed to memory practically by all ecclesiastics of the Roman Church in saying it in their Sunday Office for prime.

there were councils held, A.D. 813, at Arles, Mayence, Rheims, Tours, and Chalons, by his order, of which only the three first published any dogmatic canon at all; none of them name, and the first alone shows acquaintance with, the Athanasian Creed. (Mansi, xiv. 58.) Charlemagne himself seems to have published a capitulary, A.D. 802, headed, "Admonitio de symbolo fidei," which names no creed at all, and is purely original. (Ib. App. 267.) There is no allusion to it in the letter said to have been written by him to Leo III., from Aix, A.D. 809; (ib. 23-6;) none in the dogmatic canons passed at Paris, (ib. 536,) or Aix, (ib. 677,) or the Archbishop of Bourges, within thirty years of that time. It is named by Adalbert, Bishop of Tervan, in professing his faith to Archbishop Hincmar on his consecration: (ib. xvii. App. 426,) quoted unnamed by one bishop in England, whose date will be discussed hereafter; and for other authorities subsequently to this period, I may refer generally to Waterland's Hist. c. 2, p. 39, *et seq.*, ed. 1728.

But if the Athanasian Creed was really the work of Paulinus, how came the title which it has always borne to have been given to it? The real answer to this is, I fear, supplied by the class of testimonies remaining for examination; otherwise there would be several ways of accounting for it perfectly free from cavil. In the first place, the work was confessedly not original, but compiled. Secondly, Paulinus, had he published it himself, might have quoted numerous precedents for giving it to the world under cover of a greater name than his own. Without appealing to forgeries, had not Vigilius, Bishop of Thapsus, in Africa, published numerous works under borrowed names, including that of S. Athanasius; and were there not countless unexceptionable tracts and sermons in circulation attributed to S. Augustine that were none of his? If people were christened after their patron-saints, why should not their works be? Besides,

"Call your picture a Raphael or a Rubens, whatever its intrinsic excellencies, if you wish it to attract general notice," is what people say still. But, thirdly, Paulinus, was *not* the publisher of his own work. It was taken out of his hands by his imperial master, and appropriated to a public purpose. Well! had this stood alone, there would have been little still to explain in the course pursued. Paulinus was had in high honour by his master, and by all who knew him; but this was a limited circle after all. He was no world-wide celebrity. And Charlemagne was much too good a politician to have required the entire clergy of his dominions to learn by heart "the faith of the Patriarch Paulinus," who was then alive. Further, were there nothing else to be considered, we might recognise a touch of humour or affectation in the misnomer harmonising admirably with what we know to have been the manners of his times and court. To gratify his thirst for knowledge, he had gathered a number of learned men around him, who pursued their studies in his palace, where there was a first-rate library for those times, and formed what Mr. Hallam* calls "a sort of literary club," whose members were designated and addressed each other by assumed names. Charlemagne was called David, Alcuin Flaccus or Horace, Angilbert Homer, Arno Aquila, Riculph Damætas, Adelard Augustine, and so forth. Paulinus, in spite of his years, cannot have been the solitary exception to a rule to which Charlemagne conformed. What was his *nom de plume*? Why should it not have been Athanasius? There were several fanciful as well as well-founded analogies, patent to everybody, and highly congenial to the tastes of those days in favour of it. Aquileia was and had long been in some sense, as I have shown, the Alexandria of Italy. Paulinus, its bishop, had patriarchal rank, and this, combined

* Middle Ages, iii. 521, note, ed. 1837.

with his age, acquirements, and grave demeanour, raised him aloft on a pedestal above his fellows. Constantine, the founder of the Byzantine Empire, had his Athanasius, should not Charlemagne, the restorer of the Western, have his? Besides, it had actually happened, that as when the Consubstantiality of the Son of God with the Father was challenged, the Egyptian Athanasius stood firm when Rome failed: so when the Procession of the Holy Ghost from the Son as well as the Father was challenged, and Rome temporised once more, the Italian Athanasius headed the orthodox. Considerations like these would have been passing likely to have weighed with the members of "the club" at Aix, were there the smallest evidence that they had ever elected to call Paulinus Athanasius. Unfortunately, there is not a grain of evidence in their writings—at least, in those that have come down to us—that he was ever known to them by that name. Was he then singular in having no assumed name at all? *Or was this his assumed name known only to the initiated, and kept a profound secret from all else?* It matters little whether this was so, or whether the name of S. Athanasius was given to the Creed alone, *so long as there was concealment*. And concealment in one way or other, and for some deliberate purpose, there must have been, otherwise the origin of this Creed could not have remained so long a mystery.

This brings me to my other class of testimonies in reserve. They belong to the same period, beginning almost as soon, and extending at least as late, as the first class. But their peculiar feature is that they are wholly controversial; and not only so, but confined exclusively to one controversy—the Procession of the Holy Ghost—and that not with heretics or sectarians, but with the whole Eastern Church. As everybody knows, who knows anything of these times, the two principal questions handled by the Caroline divines were this and Adoptionism. And Adoptionism being a revival of Nestorianism, though in the rudest guise, necessitated recourse to all the arguments employed by the Fathers of the Councils of Ephesus and Chalcedon once more. Now, there were three times the number of works written against Adoptionism at least, that there were on the Procession; and by A.D. 800, with one exception, they had all been published. But in all eighth century works against Adoptionism the Athanasian Creed is never once cited or even implied as such in any way. *In this one exception,** dedicated, not to Charlemagne, but to his successor Lewis, it is.* The treatises on the Procession commence subsequently to A.D. 800; and

* Agobard adv. Fel. (or rather, a posthumous tract of Felix), c. 2: "Quia ut beatus Athanasius: ait: 'Fidem Catholicam nisi quis integram inviolatamque servaverit, absque dubio in æternum peribit.'"

of these there is not one in which the Athanasian Creed is not cited prominently by name, sometimes more than once. View these facts in connection with the complimentary letter addressed by Alcuin to Paulinus that year, and who can doubt when the Athanasian Creed was written, or by whom? Probably the earliest of these latter testimonies to it has been anticipated.* Charlemagne had for some years previously been either sending monks to Jerusalem, or else receiving monks from Jerusalem, on various errands. Three such had presented him at Rome, on the occasion of his coronation, with the keys of the Holy Sepulchre and of Calvary, together with a banner, in the name of the Patriarch.† And one such‡ was of German extraction, named Egilbald, otherwise called George, being abbot of the convent on Mount Olives, where the controversy, first known with any

---

* C. 3.   † Eginhard, A.D. 800.
‡ Annal. Laur. A.D. 807.

OF THE ATHANASIAN CREED. 245

certainty to have been agitated at Frankfort, was first revived. It was revived, as the reader may need to be reminded, by some monks of that convent singing the interpolated creed there in the hearing of the Geeks; and who defended themselves for so singing it—to the Greeks—by declaring that their faith was that of the holy Roman Church; *to the Pope, by declaring that it was so said in the Creed of S. Athanasius.* The Greeks were told that the interpolated creed represented the faith of the Roman Church; the *Pope* was confronted *with the Athanasian Creed;* a former Pope having ventured to rebuke Charlemagne for his former onslaught on their uninterpolated creed.

I have called this testimony to the existence of the Athanasian Creed *probably the earliest* of class two; and for this reason. It can hardly be doubted it was this incident on Mount Olives which made Charlemagne bid his theologians occupy themselves in writing on the Procession. Now, what the character of their works was to be appears from the dedication affixed to one of them, and their date from the address of another. Theodulph, Bishop of Orleans, says:

> " Imperii vestri, rex inclyte, jussa secutus
>   Defero Theodulphus hæc documenta libens;
> Queis Patre seu Nato procedere Spiritus almus
>   Astruitur, legis hoc reboante tubâ."

What he had been ordered to do, then, was to collect passages from the Fathers on the Procession. His work, accordingly, consists of citations from the writings of twelve Fathers—nine Latin and three Greek. Alcuin's treatise—for such it is considered to be from bearing his name in a MS. given to the church of Laon by one of its bishops named Dido, who died A.D. 891—has a dedicatory letter prefixed to it,[*] confirming in prose

---

[*] Inter quos ego ... vestrorum famulorum extremus ... sancti Evangelii et beatorum Patrum auctoritatem secutus, secundum vestræ sublimitatis jussionem, conscripsi libellum.

all that Theodulph had stated in verse, but addressing Charlemagne besides as "*Augustus.*" As Charlemagne was crowned Emperor A.D. 800, and as Alcuin died A.D. 804, this treatise to have been by Alcuin, cannot have been written earlier than the one, nor later than the other, date. In any case both treatises were written after the establishment of the empire; for "rex" in poetry, joined with "imperii," and having "Augustus" for its pendant, cannot mean less. Their reference to the Athanasian Creed might almost seem to have been traced out for them. Alcuin says in his first chapter:

"The blessed Athanasius, the most reverend Bishop of the city of Alexandria, then .... in the 'Exposition* of the Catholic faith,' which the illustrious doctor

* There is a genuine work of S. Athanasius entitled "Exposition of Faith," and in his work "Against the Heresy of Felix," c. 58, Alcuin seems to cite this; but his quotation is in reality taken from the doubtful tract "De Incarn." ascribed to S. Athanasius. (Op. iv. 30. Ed. Ben.)

himself composed, and which the universal Church professes, declares the Procession of the Holy Spirit from the Father and the Son in these words:

"The Father is made of none, neither created nor begotten. The Son is of the Father alone, not made, nor created, but begotten. The Holy Ghost is of the Father and the Son, not made, nor created, nor begotten, but proceeding."

Then, in bringing his work to a conclusion, once more:

"For, as the blessed Athanasius, Bishop of the city of Alexandria, testifies: 'Such as the Father is, such is the Son, and such is the Holy Ghost,' etc. continuing his quotation right through what he had cited before, and ending with the verse, which, of course, speaks for itself, as not having been done without meaning. '*He therefore that will be saved must thus think of the Trinity.*'" *

On reference to the work of Theo-

* Migne's Patrol. cv. 71.

dulph, it may appear to have been done with concert also: for Theodulph, in quoting from what he calls "the Creed" of S. Athanasius, to show that the Holy Ghost proceeds from the Father and the Son, begins where Alcuin had begun first, and ends where he had left off last.*

But it is Ratramn, the monk of Corbey, writing in the days of Archbishop Hincmar, who best describes the gain its publication had been to the Latins. Having designated it as "the treatise concerning the faith which S. Athanasius published, *and proposed to all Catholics for acceptance*," he continues:

"The Latin bishops, therefore, highly approving of the orthodox doctrine which it contained, and looking upon it as a singular bulwark of strength against the wicked Arian dogma—*for they perceived that it had been drawn from Scripture*—added to the symbol of the faith in speaking of the Holy Ghost, 'Who pro-

* Migne's Patrol. cv. 247.

ceedeth from the Father and the Son.' Hence it is from those days, that is, from Constantine, when the Council of the 318 Fathers met at Nicæa, down to our own times, the Western Church has ever held this faith; not that the Catholic Church of the Greeks has ever abandoned it from unwillingness to part with the true doctrine, as is declared in their works. Still it is this faith which you —the Greeks—are accusing now, moved I know not by what levity, deceived I know not by what error."

On which passage I remarked four years ago: "That in point of fact the use of the Athanasian Creed for *controversial* purposes *originated* with the Greek question; and the effect of it was to set up a fictitious antiquity for Latin doctrine, analogous to what was set up through the pseudo-Decretals for Latin discipline."*

With the evidence now before me I

* "Christendom's Divisions," ii. 430.

can come to no other conclusion than that this effect was deliberately planned by Charlemagne, and planned for a twofold purpose: first, to justify the interpolated creed to the Pope, and convict the Greeks of error in rejecting it; and secondly, to substitute "the Catholic faith of S. Athanasius" in the West, as a standard of orthodoxy, for that of Nicæa.

Charlemagne's aspirations were patent enough. He wanted to found a second Roman Empire upon a durable basis. To effect this it was necessary that every remaining tie binding the West to dependence upon the East should be weakened or dissolved. As he examined them carefully, he found them all rotten and ready to burst at a touch but one, namely, the religious tie; and even in the religious tie there was a flaw, which, by judicious straining, might be compelled to give till a rupture was effected: and this was the interpolated Creed. He saw it was as safe to be upheld by the West as to be condemned by the East. On this he lost no time in bringing pressure to bear, but at first he was foiled. How was he foiled? Having appealed to the faith of the First Nicene Council against the Second, he had been answered by no less an authority than the reigning Pope, who proved to him that the faith of both Councils was the same; who warned him also that to attack the Creed of the Second was, in effect, to incur all the penalties decreed against the smallest departure from that Creed by the Fourth Council. Any further appeal to the Nicene faith, consequently, was out of the question, was dangerous, might be fatal to the Creed of his choice. To appeal to the Creed "of the Apostles" on this point, again, was futile, as it was the least explicit of any. But the die had been cast, and Rome must be won at all costs. If Rome sided with the Greeks on a question of religion, it needed not his sagacity to foresee that his Empire would be deprived of the very prestige on which, for durable purposes, he could rely most. Under these circumstances, let us suppose that S. Athanasius had really written the Creed bearing his name, that by some mischance it had been buried in a corner till then, and then unexpectedly come to light and been placed in the hands of Charlemagne. Could he have desired anything better calculated to advance his purpose? Here was the greatest champion of Orthodoxy the Greek Church had ever produced formally stating the Procession according to the Latin view. If he could not have this, a Creed which S. Athanasius might have written, or which people might be persuaded he had, was obviously the next best thing. And this was precisely what Paulinus placed in his hands. As I have said, there were several personal reasons suggestive of the name of Athanasius, under the circumstances, as worthy to be borne by Paulinus.

Others may have commended themselves on intrinsic grounds. There was a genuine work of S. Athanasius entitled " Exposition of the Faith." And this is one of the designations applied to the Athanasian Creed by Alcuin. Again, there was a work by Vigilius, Bishop of Thapsus, on the Trinity, then circulating as a work of S. Athanasius. It is quoted as such, and in immediate connection with the Athanasian Creed, by Theodulph, to name no more. The similarity between the Athanasian Creed and this work has often been noticed: it is as if one had suggested the other. Consequently, when the former was called " The Faith of S. Athanasius," and the latter supposed to be a work of his, each would bear out the other in its fictitious title.

All these considerations may have helped to determine the naming of the Athanasian Creed, by whomsoever suggested. Admirably put together as it is, its naming achieved its success. Had it appeared as the Faith or Creed of S. Augustine, no Greek would have given it a second thought, or been at the pains of accommodating it in Greek to his own views. Accommodating it in Greek—for it found its way into Greek at last, just as the forged donation of Constantine was ultimately by the bewildered Greeks admitted into their canon law—from the unscrupulousness and assurance with which it was put forward on the Latin side. We have seen the stress laid upon its damnatory clauses by the theologians of Charlemagne. No sooner had the conquest of Constantinople been achieved by the *Latinity* which he founded, than it was, by a strange fatality, pressed upon the Greeks once more by the envoys of Gregory IX., whose collection of the *Decretals* recalls so many kindred forgeries: and this time in the old Church of Nicæa, as if in mockery of the "Nicene faith" of former ages, to whose traditionary prerogatives it had been opposed with so much success in the West. And this was the use, and this the tale, which the Popes encouraged of it then.* First, the Latin doctrine was formally stated; next, it was to be received under anathema: "Wherefore whoever believes the Holy Ghost not to proceed from the Son is in the way of perdition." Then this is justified by the Creed which S. Athanasius is stated to have composed in Latin. Whence holy Athanasius, *when an exile in the West*, in the "*Exposition of the Faith*," *which he set forth in Latin*, says: . . . "The Holy Ghost is of the Father and of the Son, not made, nor begotten, but proceeding." Nor is this all. A citation immediately follows from

---

* I quote from the formal paper which the Monks exhibited. Mansi, xxiii. 61-299, from which I inadvertently inferred in "Christendom's Divisions" ii. 430, that this Creed existed in Greek then.

the *genuine* "Exposition" of the same Saint, which, the envoys are pleased to admit, "he set forth in Greek," but where he could not for a moment be understood to say the same thing *but for the gloss put upon his genuine work by the counterfeit Creed.* The puzzled Greeks, of course, could only solve* the difficulty by evading it. And such was the prestige this secured for it by one fiction after another that, at the distance of nearly five hundred years from Charlemagne, S. Thomas Aquinas is content to appeal, in confirmation of the Latin doctrine, to it alone. "The Holy Ghost," he says, "has been thought not to proceed from the Son." Four authorities, including the Niceno-Constantinopolitan Creed in its unadulterated shape, and three arguments on the negative side follow. One authority suffices, on the affirmative side, to determine the question: "Sed contra

* See their reply, Mansi, xxiii. p. 307, *et seq.*

est quod dicit Athanasius in symbolo suo."* Such has been the success of a false title. The two golden calves never stood Jeroboam in better stead for weaning the ten tribes from Jerusalem, than the fabricated origin of this and the Apostles' Creed stood Charlemagne for weaning the West from "the Nicene faith." Let policy be measured by success alone, and this naming of the Athanasian Creed was a masterpiece. But what excuse can be made for men devoted to God, like Alcuin, like Paulinus himself, who could assist in propagating what they must have known to be a fraud and a lie? They must have known both of them, if not whose composition it was—for it may not have received its last touch from either of them —at least whose it was not. To have called it merely "the faith of S. Athanasius" need have implied no more than that in their opinion it had been fairly

* Sum. Theol. I. 9. xxxvi. art. 2.

culled from his works. But to assent to speak of it, like Alcuin, as having been actually composed by him, only shows how degradingly subservient the best of men in those days were to a monarch against whose falsifications of fact they no more dared protest, than his offences against morality reprove.

He was their "David;" but though he was a greater sinner than David in many ways, they never credit him with any of David's sins. He was their Pope; they neither consulted nor deferred to anybody besides him. As he commanded, so they wrote; what they wrote, they submitted to his correction; and when he bade them do this for themselves, they protested it would have been far better done by him.* "For one thousand

* Alcuin, Ep. ci. ed. Migne. "Gratias agimus venerandæ pietati vestræ quod libellum vestræ jussionis præceptum, vobis directum, auribus sapientiæ vestræ recitari fecistis; et quod notare jussistis errata illius, et remisistis ad corrigendum, quamvis a vobis melius emendare potuisset: quia

years," as I *stated the fact* elsewhere, "the Latin Church has been committed, through them, to the theological *ipse dixit* of a secular autocrat, as lax in practice as Henry VIII. on divorce and marriage: as sanguinary, when it suited his purpose, as Eccelin da Romano, son-in-law of Frederic II., great in intellect and great in arms, but unscrupulous and impatient of any control short of his own will in both."* If we should say that the damnatory clauses of the Athanasian Creed were dictated by him originally, or inserted with his own hand in revising it, we should probably not be far wrong. Nothing was published by his gravest theologians without his *imprimatur;* and his own words to the bishops of Spain in epitomising "the Catholic faith" for their edification are: "This

alterius judicium in quolibet opere plus sæpissimè valet quam proprii auctoris." The qualification in this last sentence is wanting elsewhere. He is here speaking of his work against Felix.

* "Christendom's Divisions," ii. 548.

orthodox faith handed down by the Apostles its teachers, and by the universal Church preserved, we for our part and ability profess to maintain *and preach* everywhere entire: seeing that in any besides this, which the Church has always from the beginning peacefully and unanimously kept, there is no salvation;" * or, as he puts it in the Caroline Books, affirmatively: " This is the true faith: this profession we hold and maintain: he who keeps this unconfused and undefiled will have eternal salvation." † In both cases he is speaking, not of the creeds, but of a dogmatic summary drawn up by himself of what he thought everybody bound to believe; pronouncing on some points where the creeds were reserved, and defining some that had never formed part of any creed at all. And this tone he forced upon or encouraged in others. Reference was made some pages ago to a formula which the reign-

* Mansi, xiii. 900.   † iii. 1.

ing Pope, Leo III. submitted to him before sending into the East. I pointed out that it contained stronger expressions in favour of the Latin view of the Procession than are to be found in the extant writings of any Pope for the next four hundred years; and that it ends with a damnatory clause likewise: "Him that believes not according to this faith, the holy Catholic and Apostolic Church condemns." As Leo had accepted a synodical letter from the Patriarch of Constantinople, in which the Greek view of the Procession is laid down only two years before, and as he that same year also peremptorily declined authorising the insertion of the "*Filioque*" into the Creed, if he really penned those sentences on the Procession, he cannot surely be supposed to have penned the anathema, with which his letter at present stands credited. But the reasons against crediting Paulinus with the damnatory clauses of the Athanasian Creed are still more cogent.

In general, no doubt, the Athanasian Creed is a compilation, as I have intimated already, and shall substantiate in detail further on: but there are portions of it which fit Paulinus so well, that in fact they could be attributed to nobody with more reason.

1. Of these the verse relating to the Procession of the Holy Ghost is most conspicuous. It is literally moderation itself. Few advocates of the Latin doctrines would have been content to stop where it stops; few Greeks, as a contributor to Macmillan observed four years ago,* would have declined going as far. The Holy Ghost is described as "of the Father and of the Son," first—the preposition used being *a*, not *ex*: and then "neither made, nor created, nor begotten, but proceeding?" The copula, rigidly supplied in the two previous verses, is altogether wanting in this. The words may imply, but they notably stop short

* For Nov., p. 24.

of asserting, that "the Holy Ghost *proceeds* from the Son" in the Latin sense—"*ex* Patre Filioque procedit."

An explanation of this studied moderation is as plainly wanting, as it is plainly supplied in the address of Paulinus to the Synod of Friuli, just one year after Pope Adrian had vindicated the faith of the Seventh Council against Charlemagne, A.D. 796. Part of what I am about to quote from this address has been anticipated. Nobody can read it as a whole without feeling that the speaker is acting the part of apologist for somebody throughout who had gone too far, had been called to account, and reproved. " Far be it from us," he says, " and *from every faithful heart*, either to compose or teach a different faith or creed: or differently from what they enjoined." He is quoting the very Canon which the Pope bade his master beware of violating. There had been no violation, he contends, of this canon when the "*Filioque*" was inserted. Nobody blamed the Constantinopolitan Fathers for having enlarged the Creed of Nicæa. The words "and from the Son," had been added on similar grounds to their creed. When, and by whose authority they were added, and against what heretics, he omits to state: and this he cannot conceal is his weak point. Perplexed with his subject, he at length bursts forth as already stated in the strain of compromise before quoted: "How Catholic those Fathers who grounded in faith unwavering have confessed the Holy Spirit to proceed from the Father: how glorious those likewise, who have confessed Him to proceed from the Son as well."*

He who said that, unquestionably would have been not the least likely to

---

* Compare with this the Conf. of Faith ascribed to Alcuin, iii. 22, where, after arguing in favour of the Latin view, he proceeds: " Et ideò *non aliâ, non diversâ,* sed *unâ eâdemque* fide, credo et in Spiritum Sanctum, Dominum et vivificantem, Qui ex Patre Filioque procedit," etc.

have written this: "The Holy Ghost, of the Father and the Son: not made, nor created, nor begotten, but proceeding;" yet would have been the least likely to have added: "He, therefore, *that will be saved*, must thus think of the Trinity." Granting accordingly that Paulinus composed the first, who could have composed the second? Alcuin and Theodulph, writing by order of Charlemagne, both terminate their citations from the Athanasian Creed with this verse, as I have remarked already: the Caroline Books themselves say: "This is the true faith ... he who keeps this unconfused and undefiled will have eternal salvation:" which amounts practically to the same thing. On the other hand, Charlemagne never once quotes the Athanasian Creed himself.

How is all this to be explained? The teaching of the Athanasian Creed on the Procession was too moderate for Charlemagne: yet, such as it was, it may have seemed calculated to answer his purpose better than any thing more pronounced. He let it stand then, on the principle of utilising the thin edge of the wedge. He let it stand yet so as to put outside the pale of salvation everybody who believed less—and hence supplemented it with *words of his own to that effect*. As it was not strong enough doctrine for him, he never appealed to it himself: but its very moderation might convince the Pope: and this, asserted under pain of salvation, confound the Greeks. His monks from Mount Olives, accordingly, were instructed to refer to it in excusing themselves *to* the one; his theologians to press it *against* the others with stress laid on the particular clause most likely to frighten them into submission.

Whatever the reader may think of this explanation, the almost verbal identity between the passage lately quoted from the Caroline Books, and the central of the damnatory clauses in the Athanasian

Creed is a simple fact; central, I say, to distinguish it from two more standing at the beginning and end; making three in all. Similarly, that which stands at the end: "This is the Catholic faith, which except a man believe faithfully and firmly he cannot be saved," cannot but recall what Charlemagne, writing to the Bishops of Spain, had said of his own summary: "This orthodox faith .... we profess to maintain and preach everywhere entire, seeing that there is no salvation in any besides it."

What is, as it were, prefixed to the Creed, was a general axiom of those days founded on the verse which says "Without faith"—which everybody thought meant dogma then—"it is impossible to please God." Its specific application to the dogmatism which follows is riveted by the other two.

The teaching of the Athanasian Creed, then, on the Procession apart from those damnatory clauses at the middle and end,

I contend goes far to fix it upon Paulinus, the moment his name is mentioned in connexion with it, and his history told.

2. Nor can I think my next instance less cogent, provided our previous associations are dismissed in examining it. From constantly repeating the Athanasian Creed, we have got the doctrine engrained into us that "all men will rise with *their own bodies*;" but there was a time when this was explicitly taught nowhere but in the Aquileian Church. "Ecclesia nostra," says Rufinus, "quæ quod a cæteris traditur, 'carnis resurrectionem:' uno addito pronomine tradidit, '*hujus* carnis resurrectionem."'* Anybody who will be at the pains of comparing the various professions and dogmatic summaries extant previous to the ninth century, will find that wherever this doctrine is *expressed*, it can be traced more or less directly to the Creed of Aquileia. This fact, consequently, would go far to connect the

* § 43.

author of the Athanasian Creed with that Church in some way.

3. One of the longest and most involved verses of the Athanasian Creed is the following—in our English version it forms two: " For like as we are compelled by the Christian verity to acknowledge every Person by Himself to be God and Lord, so we are forbidden by the Catholic religion to say, there be three Gods or three Lords."

The matter of this is, doubtless, to be found in S. Augustine: but Waterland's parallels* fail him here completely for *the turn of the sentence*, which is just what is supplied in the thirteenth chapter of the first book of his work against Felix by Paulinus himself, in arguing from the Trinity to the Incarnation. "For just as in the Mystery of the Holy Trinity, by the distinction of Three Persons, and the inseparable majesty of one and the same glorious

* Hist., p. 234.

Essence, one God is believed on by us, not three: so, in the dispensation of the great and holy sacrament of the Mediator of God and man, the Man Christ Jesus, by the real distinction of two Natures, and profession of the truth of one Person, the rule of Apostolic faith at once prompts and incites us to believe sincerely with the heart unto righteousness, and to confess healthfully with the mouth unto salvation, not Two Sons, Two Gods, or Two Christs, but One and the same Christ Jesus, of either, and in either Nature, the True and Only-begotten Son of God, the True and Almighty God."

4. This passage, for matter again, might have been quoted for another purpose. It occurs, as has been said, in a work against Adoptionism; it, therefore, connects the author of the Creed with the author of this treatise, by showing that Adoptionism is specifically condemned in the Creed.

Compare this passage, for instance, with the following verse:

"Who, although He be God and Man, yet He is not two, but one Christ.

"One: not by conversion of the Godhead into Flesh, but by taking of the manhood into God.

"One altogether: not by confusion of Substance, but by unity of Person." . . .

Putting the question of their authorship out of sight, both cannot but have been directed against the same error. Waterland, from connecting these verses with the older heresies of Nestorius and Eutyches, instead of their revival, such as it was, by Felix, is hopelessly puzzled to decide when, and by whom, and with what object this Creed could have been written.*

I sum up what I venture to think has been established on each of these points:

* Hist., c. vii.

1. Its age and authorship have been established from hence—A.D. 800 Alcuin compliments Paulinus in a glowing letter addressed to him on having supplied a great need by a recent work of his, which is thereupon described in terms hardly capable of being improved upon had he been describing this Creed.

Within a year of that time a work bearing a name by which this Creed was afterwards known for centuries is, by Alcuin's master, ordered to serve the very purpose which Alcuin had declared this work of Paulinus admirably fitted to serve so recently, and to which he had been directing his master's attention for some time before. Alcuin himself cites this Creed, a year later, for the first and only time in his life, dying the year following. It is cited freely by others thenceforward, never having been cited in any document earlier than A.D. 800. This, indeed, has to be further proved. The Creed itself contains strong grounds for

T

fixing its authorship upon Paulinus, and nothing to the contrary.

2. The object embodied in it has been shown to be twofold, by distinguishing between its compiler and publisher. Paulinus, in compiling it, simply meant to supply what had been so long discussed, but never achieved: a dogmatic compendium of the Catholic faith in opposition to the errors then prevalent, or supposed to be prevalent, over and above the Creeds. Charlemagne, in publishing it, had another purpose besides this in view, which determined its title—a title probably suggested to him, in the first instance, by its being a work by Paulinus. This other purpose is revealed not in its title only, but in the uses to which he turned it.

First of all, he caused it to be quoted simultaneously, both against the Greeks, and to the Pope, with the object of vindicating the "*Filioque*" which King Reccared had inserted in the Niceno-

Constantinopolitan Creed, and which he, for reasons best known to himself, had taken under his special patronage. Next, he decreed that "the faith of S. Athanasius"—namely, this Creed—should be learnt by heart everywhere by his clergy. The significance of this act is strikingly brought out by contrast. His father Pepin, following all other precedents elsewhere till then, decreed that the "Nicene faith" should be preached throughout his whole realm. Charlemagne, from having quarrelled with the Second Nicene Council, and discovered that it was his own creed really which was in fault, abstained from ever referring to "the Nicene faith" in those capitularies which he published as King, and overtly substituted for it "the faith of S. Athanasius" in those which he published as Emperor. He thus adopted "the faith of S. Athanasius" as his standard of orthodoxy. In this he was followed slowly but surely by the Popes, who received it at his bidding into their Breviary, and used it against the Greeks with a shrewdness which in this case was not their own; and by the schoolmen also, who saw in it their best argument for the Latin doctrines, both alike testifying to the surpassing foresight and sagacity with which a document so framed had been so called and utilised. This, then, is the solution of the mystery that has so long enveloped the Athanasian Creed. It was at once the expression of Latin dogmatism, and the lever of Latin despotism: a symbol of the impending subjugation of the Church of Christ, both in thought and act, to a spirit which was neither of Jerusalem, nor yet of Greece, but of Rome—of Rome first pagan, and then Christian. Every time we recite the Athanasian Creed, it is reason not Scripture that speaks: Charlemagne not Athanasius that expounds: a faith deliberately set up in opposition to the faith of Nicæa and Constantinople that is professed. All this is incontrovertible, unless the facts which have been adduced are not facts. In discussing its structure, we shall be brought face to face with the sole ground for challenging them: namely, that of its pre-existence.

CHAPTER V.

THE ATHANASIAN CREED A COMPILATION, NOT AN ORIGINAL WORK.

THE detection of the spuriousness of its title was not, of course, sufficient in itself to establish the comparatively late origin of the Athanasian Creed; and its intrinsic merits as a composition, or a conservative feeling in general, may have predisposed many to stop short of that, and to welcome testimonies to its antiquity from whatsoever quarter without cross-examining them. Such testimonies range themselves under three heads — 1. External testimonies in which it is named; or, 2. Manuscripts in which it is transcribed, as such; and, 3. Passages cited from it in appearance, but without naming it, in other works.

I shall dispose of the two former of these very summarily. First, they are discredited in general, and one and all equally, by the threefold fact that it is nowhere cited by Alcuin and his contemporaries before A.D. 800 : that he himself hailed the appearance of just such a work in that year by the most celebrated of his friends as a public boon; and that from A.D. 800 onwards not only was the Athanasian Creed cited by him and by others as such, but it was turned to the very purpose, which on his own showing he knew of no work at all calculated to serve, previously to perusing that of his friend. Alcuin, if the expression may be allowed, literally let the cat out of the bag in disclosing this.

Secondly, there is no MS. of it or testimony to it before then extant that can be relied on : in short, the more remote the date assigned to them, the more delusive they have been found. Even so, the earliest testimony still cited has never been supposed earlier than the end of the sixth century. Here again I regret having to find fault, in the interest of students, with Professor Heurtley's editorship; and complain of there being so much to mislead them in a work especially planned for their benefit. One of the tracts reprinted by him is a commentary on the Athanasian Creed, with this heading: " Venantii Honorii Fortunati, Pictavensis Episcopi, fidei Catholicæ Expositio?"* And this is his introduction to it: " The tract of Venantius Fortunatus is a commentary on the Athanasian Creed; and it supplies the earliest external testimony to the date of that formulary. Venantius was .... still living in the year 600. His commentary may be dated at about the year 570."†

So far as these remarks are concerned, the Professor is merely repeating Waterland, and Waterland‡ Muratori; but his

---

* " De Fide et S." p. 153.   † Ibid. p. 40.
‡ C. iii. p. 60; Comp. 293, *et seq.*

heading is in advance of both, and of all others. In the first MS. that came to light containing it this commentary was found without any heading at all, and was so printed by Zaccaria.* Muratori discovered it in another with this heading: " Expositio fidei Catholicæ Fortunati."† Waterland, in another, with this: " Expositio in fide Catholica." And no other transcript of it, to the best of my belief, has since been found. If so, what justification can the Professor offer of his *new* heading? Should he not first have satisfied himself that Muratori was right in singling the well-known Bishop of Poitiers out of all the many Fortunatuses that figure in his collection of Italian records as *the* Fortunatus of this commentary. Certainly, the one reason which seems to have weighed with him is not convincing. The MS. containing it, and attributing it to *a* Fortunatus, contained another tract,

* Excurs. Lit., p. 507.
† Anec. ii. 212, *et seq.*

entitled "Exposition of the Creed by Fortunatus the Presbyter," which Exposition proved identical with that of the Bishop of Poitiers, occurring in the eleventh book of his Miscellanies. This tract has been noticed in a former chapter. But Muratori should have reflected that there is nothing in either the Miscellanies or any known work of the Bishop of Poitiers indicating his acquaintance with the Athanasian Creed, let alone this commentary; moreover, that his own MS. contained two more commentaries on the Athanasian Creed besides this, one of them with the same heading, *minus* the word "Fortunati," which Waterland's MS. omits too; further, that the word "Fortunati," strictly construed, would make Fortunatus author of the Creed, and not its commentator, as he himself admits; and, lastly, that this commentary contains several extracts from Alcuin. Waterland, from his MS. omitting these, was put on his guard, and bracketted them as interpolations. Who shall say they were not quotations? The tract is made up of extracts all through. And it so happens that there was a rather energetic Fortunatus, Patriarch of Grado, and second of that name, who was employed by the son and successor of Charlemagne to negotiate with the East, A.D. 824, and died afterwards in France.* Who more likely to have occupied himself with the Athanasian Creed, and quoted Alcuin, and been transcribed, if he left anything behind him in writing, by French hands? At any rate, the most recent editors of the works of the Bishop of Poitiers have decided upon internal evidence, as well they might, that this commentary can be none of his.†

* "Vir inquieti animi," says Pagi, (ad Baron. A.D. 824, n. 9,) "qui tamen multis in rebus laudem meruit, ut videre est apud Sigon. Lib. iv., de Regn. Ital. et Ughell. Tom. v. Ital. Sac. in Patriarch. Grad."

† "Auctores Hist. Lit. Franc. inficiantur illam Expositionem nostri Fortunati fetum esse : quorum

Its author may have stolen from the author of the beautiful hymns "Ave Maris Stella" and "Vexilla Regis Prodeunt," as well as from others; but, to judge from this specimen, and in the absence of any more direct proof, he was clearly not *that* Fortunatus.

Passing by the now-acknowledged spurious letter of S. Isidore to Duke Claud, which imposed on Bishop Pearson,* but which, by referring to the Athanasian Creed in the same breath with the strife which it asserts to have been then raging on the Procession, tells us in so many words why it should have been antedated by two centuries, and assigned to S. Isidore: we come to the

---

sententiæ ut meam adjungam facit stylus," etc. Michael Angelo Luchi ad Venant. Fort. ap. Migne, Patrol. lxxxviii. 586.

* "As in the Creed attributed to S. Athanasius, which though we cannot say was his, yet we know was extant about the year 600, by the Epistle of Isidorus Hispalensis, 'ad Claudium Ducem.'" On the Creeds, ii. 193, Oxford Ed.

last remaining of the stock-passages hitherto relied on: a canon of Autun, as it has been called, which runs thus:

"That any presbyter, deacon, subdeacon, or clerk not reciting the Creed which the Apostles by inspiration of the Holy Ghost delivered, and the Faith of the holy prelate Athanasius, satisfactorily, be condemned by the bishop."

This canon has been assigned to a Synod of Autun, said to have been held A.D. 640, under S. Leodegar. Assigned; but on what grounds? Simply that it was discovered two centuries and a half ago by Sirmondus, in a collection of canons at the Abbey of S. Benignus in Dijon,* under this heading, "Canones Augustodunenses Era I." What this heading may mean is one thing; and what credit may be due to this collection another. To judge of the latter correctly, till it has been printed entire, or impartially described by a competent

* Concil. Gall. i. 507.

critic, is out of the question. All the notice given of it by Sirmondus is confined to this canon. A collection of the same kind has come to light more recently, and been printed in Paris, but in part only, named, after the owner or discoverer of the MS. containing it, the Herovall Collection.* Morinus appears to have seen this at Angers, about the time when Sirmondus may have been making extracts from the other at Dijon; and Sirmondus, in the course of his researches, to have seen both. From the single remark he volunteers on the subject, we are left to infer that they were duplicate copies—and not the only copies that he had seen either—of the same collection.† But he

* Reprinted from Petit in Migne's Patrol. xcix. 991. Because M. Petit printed this collection in the same volume with Archbishop Theodore's Penitentiale, Professor Brewer, by a strange oversight, speaks of this canon as *in* the Penitentiale. Athanasian Creed, p. 5, note.

† Concil. Gall. i. 506; in his note, p. 620, he quotes, "Consensio domini Leodegari episcopi Augustodunensis," as inscribed in the last place

cannot have examined them with much care. Fortunately, we have the means of examining the Herovall collection for ourselves, so far as it has been printed. M. Petit, its editor, as I learn through Abbe Migne, whose Patrology contains it, infers its antiquity from the absence of any reference in it to the False Decretals. As it could not well have referred to them had it been compiled only the year before their publication, no higher antiquity than the latter half of the ninth century can be claimed for any part of it on that score; while by appealing to the decrees of two legendary synods under Popes Gelasius and Silvester, one part of it directly negatives its own antiquity beyond the earlier half. Again, we have two lists of canons given at the beginning and end of this collection, which by no

of several "codices," including those of Angers and Dijon. As the reading is different in the Herovall Collection, he is probably quoting from that of Dijon. Of its import he offers no intelligible explanation whatever.

means square with each other.* The one said to be prefixed to it is the longer and later of the two, and contains several references—" Canones Romanorum," for instance—not found in the other. By its own confession it must have been made subsequently to the pontificate of Gregory III., or A.D. 741, whose decrees it includes. In both, however, with a single exception, the style throughout is the same, and the number of bishops supposed to have been present at each of the synods whose canons are cited, is carefully specified: *e.g.* " the Nicene canons of 318 bishops," and so forth. The single exception occurs last of all on the longer list, and runs thus: "*Canones Augustodunenses sancti Leodegari episcopi.*" Now, it so happens that there never was but one canon of Autun supposed to be cited in this collection at all, namely, the canon in question; and with it the first chapter

---

* Both printed in p. 1076, the longer one in a note.

of this collection begins. On the other hand, there is no mention of any canons of Autun whatever in the shorter list; but what it ends with is: " Consensio et confirmatio Leodegari episcopi." What can this possibly mean? It means unquestionably that this collection was, *in its original shape*, framed during the lifetime of Bishop Leodegar—when he would not, of course, be styled " saint," and received his approval and confirmation. That additions were made to it *subsequently to his death* is attested by the longer list, where he is styled " saint." No canons of Autun were named in the shorter list, because this collection originally contained none: though Autun, in one sense, appropriated all the others, on their being confirmed there. When the canon in question was inserted, it was placed *at the head of the collection*, and being placed there was designated, " Canon Augustodunensis æra I.," as being first of a collection confirmed by the saint and former bishop of that See. The entry with which the new list of contents closed, " Canones Augustodunenses sancti Leodegari episcopi," was conceived in the same spirit. The African canons had been named by Dionysius Exignus, " canons of the Synod of the Africans at Carthage:* the fact being that they had been framed at eighteen or more different synods, but were subsequently collected and confirmed at one—that of Carthage, A.D. 419. Individual canons, on the same principle, were not unfrequently cited as canons of Carthage, though they had been framed at Hippo. Why the interpolator chose the first place for the canon in question is explained easily. The first chapter of this collection is entitled " De fide et symbolo ; " and the next canon quoted in it is that of the Third Council of Toledo prescribing the

* "Which enacted"—he continues, using the singular number—" 138 Canons." In his preface he speaks of it as " Africanum Concilium."

NOT AN ORIGINAL WORK. 291

recital in church of the Niceno-Constantinopolitan Creed, "according to the form of the Eastern churches." I have called attention already to the marked preference given in the capitularies of Charlemagne to the Apostles' and Athanasian Creeds over the Nicene. Canons enjoining their use would accordingly, by those who obeyed him, have precedence given them over canons enjoining its use. This circumstance serves of itself to indicate both the origin and age of the canon. It was one, doubtless, of the many canons framed in the ninth century, whether at Autun or elsewhere, to give effect to the "General Capitulary," published A.D. 802, where the learning by heart of the "Catholic faith of S. Athanasius," is as we have seen, first enjoined. To assign an earlier date to this canon, would be to suppose that what this capitulary prescribed had been law in France long before, and that Alcuin at Tours was ignorant of what every clerk at Autun had not so long since been in the habit of learning by heart.

One word, in conclusion, on the term "æra." To our ears it may sound familiar enough: but, as is well-known, it had a barbarous origin, having come out first in Spain, and marked a basis of computation then in use there, but which never was current out of Spain. Its meaning in these remote times, therefore, should not be too hastily assumed. "Æra," for instance, some have taken for granted, is here equivalent to canon or number one. This it may be now and then, where the reckonings in and out of Spain happen to coincide: but who can assume their agreement in all cases beforehand? Taking this collection as a specimen, we have "Canon Toletanus æra 2—" and the canon referred to, doubtless, *is* canon 2—not, however, of every Council of Toledo in succession, but of the Third of those Councils only. Further on, we have "Canon Aurelianensis æra 1," for what is really " Concil. Aurelian. iii. can. 1 ; " and again, " Canon Arausicanus æra 28," for what is " Concil. Araus. i. can. 29 : " similarly, " Canon Araus. æra 24," for " Concil. Araus. i. can. 25 : " " Canon Aurelian. æra 4," for "Concil. Aurel. iii.:" and "Canon Aurel. iv. æra 9" for Concil Aurel. v. can. 12." There was a method in use likewise, mentioned by S. Isidore, for taking account of the parallel passages of the Gospels, where canons and æras figured, and where the obscurity that enshrouds their meaning ought to deter everybody from reckoning upon it as certain in other cases.*

* Etym. vi. 15. " De canonibus Evangeliorum." His words are : " Sunt canones numero decem ; quorum primus continet numerus in quibus quatuor (Evangelistæ) eadem dixerunt, etc. . . . quorum expositio hæc est. Per singulos Evangelistas numerus quidam capitulis affixus adjacet, quibus numeris subdita est æra quædam minio notata, quæ indicat in quoto canone positus sit numerus cui subjecta est æra. Verbi gratiâ : si est æra prima, in primo canone : si secunda, in secundo : si tertia in tertio : et sic per ordinem usque ad decimum perveniens."....

In quitting these testimonies, let me append a noteworthy passage from Waterland illustrating a connection which I fully agree with him exists between the first and third.

"This comment of Fortunatus," he says, "is a great confirmation of what hath been above cited from the Council of Autun; for if the Creed was noted enough to deserve a comment upon it so early as the year 570, no wonder we find it strongly recommended by that Council in the year 670, a hundred years after. *And it is observable that as that Council recommends the Apostolical and Athanasian Creeds, without saying a word of the Nicene*, so Fortunatus, before them, comments upon those two only, taking no notice of the third."

Had Waterland only noticed the *substitution of the faith of S. Athanasius and of the Apostles*, for the Nicene, to which I have called attention, in the Caroline Capitularies, his own concluding observation would have inspired him with truer notions of both the one and the other.

There is one more document that I will notice, though it is rarely put forward. I mean the profession said to have been made by Denebert Bishop of Worcester, on his consecration, A.D. 799, to Archbishop Athelard; which, as Waterland says, "contains," but without naming it, " a considerable part of the Athanasian Creed,"* viz., from the commencement to the verse, "So that in all things, as is aforesaid, the Trinity in Unity, and the Unity in Trinity, is to be worshipped;" stopping notably short of the damnatory clause which follows. This is not difficult to explain. Hearne, whose collection contains it, supplies a number of similar professions by bishops in England of the same date; but of these there is not one containing anything at all similar to that of Bishop Denebert; though

* Ibid. p. 157.

several other bishops speak of having learnt their professions equally from the same source, viz., the teaching of their predecessors.* The uniqueness of his profession therefore consists in his quotation. Who had put it into his mouth? Why not Alcuin? Alcuin had many disciples in England, of whom Denebert may have been one; was always corresponding with them; and would be sure to give them the earliest intelligence of a new work by Paulinus. When he wrote to express his admiration of it to its author, it had not been named—perhaps contained no damnatory clauses at all, but the first. And Alcuin may have simultaneously quoted the first half of it as a specimen to Denebert, whose consecration was impending—for the dates in each case are too close, without either

---

* *E.g.* a bishop of Hereford says: "Insuper etiam et orthodoxam, Catholicam, Apostolicamque fidem, sicut ab illis didici, paucis verbis exponam," which is word for word what Denebert says of his. Text. Roff. p. 270. Comp. p. 251.

being fixable to a year, to present any difficulty*—and Denebert have quoted it to his Primate. In this case it would seem to have been first used, for public purposes, in England, *but in part only*, *and not under a forged name.*

The witness of MSS. to the antiquity of the Athanasian Creed has been both over-rated and over-stated. Negative proof is the only proof really supplied by MSS. MSS. may prove that they themselves cannot be older than a given period: they can never *prove* themselves as old: the possibility, or probability, greater or less, that they may be as old, is as much as can ever be deduced from them on the constructive side. Take, for instance, the Lombardic and the Anglo-Saxon charac-

---

* Alcuin's letter, for instance, may have been written a year sooner; or Denebert's consecration a year later. Denebert was among the subscribers to the Synod of Cloveshoe, A.D. 803, and Athelard's decree of the same year; (Wilkins, i. 167-8;) but not to the Synod of Baccauceld, A.D. 798. No intermediate subscriptions have been preserved.

ters, on which stress is apt to be laid in this instance. The use of the Lombardic would not in any case prove a MS. older than the sixth nor the Anglo-Saxon than the seventh century. But the Anglo-Saxon continued to be written after the Conquest for some time; and the Lombardic must have been in full swing one hundred years earlier. "We Lombards," said Liutprand, Bishop of Cremona, to the Emperor of Constantinople, A.D. 968, "disdain to be called Romans; so much so, that 'Roman' is the bitterest term of reproach that we can apply to our enemies: under the word 'Roman' we comprehend all that is ignoble, craven, miserly, degenerate, false, vicious."* When so much of the Lombardic spirit was unextinguished, it is not likely the Lombardic character even in ordinary writing had fallen into disuse. Take, again, the handwritings of the reigns of Edward I. and Queen Elizabeth respectively, which are

* Ap. Baron. A.D. 968, n. 23.

within everybody's reach. A MS. of the first kind could not be set down older than the thirteenth century; nor of the second kind than the sixteenth. But both styles prevailed for upwards of a century; and either could, of course, be imitated at any time subsequently to its own, where there was a reason for using it. Previously to the introduction of printing, there would naturally be more reason, as well as greater facility, for imitation. Volumes were not so easily multiplied, but that everybody was bent on utilising every blank leaf in those he possessed already; while, most of these being works of art, taste alone would dictate that there should be no great discrepancy noticeable between the performances of the later and the earlier scribe. This, again, when everybody who could write at all, was a scribe by profession, would not be so difficult to ensure as now—caligraphy being then studied in all its different styles with as much interest as architecture.

To apply these remarks to the earliest MSS. exhibiting copies of the Athanasian Creed: neither the use of the Lombardic nor of the Anglo-Saxon characters would of itself prove them earlier than the tenth or eleventh centuries, though it *would prove* them later than the sixth or seventh, and would not be inconsistent with their being of any date between the one and the other. Most, again, of the MSS. in question are Psalters, which were complete in themselves, and not at first intended to include more. Hymns and Canticles obtained admission in them as they were composed, and became popular, were taken into the Service, or both: the Athanasian Creed among them, and in general placed last. Sometimes they formed a separate appendix; sometimes were written on parchment of a different quality from what had gone before; sometimes showed a different style of handwriting, obviously later. If, occasionally, they were written on identical membranes, and in the same handwriting with the rest of the volume, careful inspection of the Calendar or of the Litanies would, in most cases, alone suffice to prevent any conclusion being drawn from such uniformity: since it would have to be extended to the confessedly later insertions in these, no less. So much for the MSS. themselves. On the other hand, if we turn to accounts given of them at various times by the learned men who have examined them, we are confronted with numerous instances in which their antiquity has been overstated only to be abandoned on closer investigation, and not one where it has ever been placed beyond doubt. "The oldest we have heard of," says Waterland, "is one mentioned by Archbishop Ussher, which he had seen in the Cotton Library, and which he judged to come up to the age of Gregory the Great." But Waterland himself disposed of this summarily by observing "that there is not at this day in the Cotton Library any such MS. copy of the Athanasian Creed, nor indeed any Latin Psalter, that can come up to the age of Gregory, or near it:"* a remark said to be as true now as then. Waterland appeals with more confidence to two MSS. vouched for by a French divine named Antelmi, one called the Treves MS., and another purporting to have been copied from it in the Colbertine Collection. But he again assigns them a date two hundred years later than M. Antelmi. Besides, he has forgotten to notice what Montfaucon told Muratori personally, viz., that he thought neither MS. earlier than the reign of Charlemagne.† The character of the Treves MS. is Lombardic; of that in the Colbertine Collection Anglo-Saxon; and the latter, from its Anglo-Saxon character alone, Montfaucon would ascribe to the eighth century. But when Muratori,

* Crit. Hist., c. iv.
† Murat. Anec. ii. 224.

NOT AN ORIGINAL WORK. 303

similarly, decided that a MS. in the Ambrosian Library, where he was librarian, belonged at least to the seventh century, from its characters being Lombardic, Montfaucon, who was shown over this collection by him, and had a high respect for his authority, placed it a century later, without hesitation.* The fact is, neither from the use of the Lombardic, nor of the Anglo-Saxon characters *alone*, should we be justified in concluding any MSS. to belong to one century more than another, between the sixth and eleventh centuries.

The Vienna MS., as it is called, has special claims of its own, which are well worth dissecting. Waterland speaks of it† as "the famous manuscript of Charles the Great, at the end of a Gallican Psalter, written in letters of gold, and presented by Charlemagne, while only King of France, to Pope Adrian I. at

---

* Crit. Hist., p. 98, Notes.
† Ibid. p. 101.

his first entrance upon the pontificate, in the year 772. Lambecius, in his catalogue of the Emperor's library at Vienna, where this MS. is, gives a large account of it." I need hardly say that Waterland in describing it is only transcribing Lambecius. But Lambecius is easily convicted on his own showing of assuming what he ought to have proved. He draws his conclusion from the dedicatory verses in gold letters on folio 1.* But these might have been written by *any* King Charles, on giving this Psalter to *any* Pope Adrian. There is nothing in them whatever to prove that the donor was Charles the Great, or the recipient Adrian I. Again, they are very inferior in point of style to the epitaph given a few pages on,† and said to have been composed by Charlemagne for this Pope. Further, there is, besides these dedicatory

* Comment. de Bibl. Cæs. Vindob. ii. 5, pp. 261-98.
† Ib. p. 265.

verses, an attestation by a notary of the empire prefixed to this Psalter, declaring that it had been used by Hildegard, wife of Charlemagne, during her life-time; and given by him after her death, and in memory of her, to the Church of Bremen on nominating S. Willehad to that See. This Lambecius of course found hard to reconcile with the dedicatory verses, *as he had interpreted them ;* it ought to have set him upon another tack. Hildegard, whose name is everything in this attestation, only became queen herself in the year in which Adrian I. became Pope. It could not, therefore, have been given to him in that year, if she used it during her life-time as queen. And as she died A.D. 783, and S. Willehad became bishop of the Church of Bremen only four or five years later, the probability is, surely, that Charlemagne, entertaining any regard for her memory, would not have parted with it at all in the interim. Besides had this attestation been written *after* a Pope had possessed it, would not his use of it have been a fact for commemoration equally with its use by the queen?

On the other hand, suppose this attestation to have been prefixed to it by the authorities of the Church of Bremen shortly after they became possessed of it, and that it was taken out of their hands in another generation to be sent to Rome, and all is plain. The dedicatory verses savour of the age of Charles the Bald infinitely more than of Charlemagne; and *Charles the Bald* was no more than *King* of France when *Adrian II.* became *Pope*. Several letters passed between them on that occasion. Add this further consideration which Lambecius himself supplies. He says that the Athanasian Creed is one of thirteen canticles contained in *an appendix* to the Psalter in question. He does not, indeed, state whether the parchment or handwriting of the appendix differs in any way from that of the Psalter; but he would scarcely have called it an appendix, had he considered it to have formed part of the Psalter originally. Further, he tells us that the title given to the " Te Deum " in this appendix, is " Hymnus quem S. Ambrosius et S. Augustinus invicem condiderunt;" to the Creed, " Symbolum sanctorum Apostolorum ;" to this, " Fides S. Athanasii episcopi Alexandrini." None of these titles are older than the ninth century; and it was sometime before they got into general use even then.

The earliest copies of the Athanasian Creed that I have seen myself have been in Psalters; but except where the Psalters are confessedly none of the earliest themselves, their age was a question altogether independent of that of the Creed. The Creed was written in different characters, on different parchment, or both; and formed part of a collection of prayers and hymns at the end of the volume, that from having found their way into the

Breviary, or become popular in convents, had at length been bound up with the Psalter. The venerable Psalter among the Cotton MS.* in the British Museum, known as "Augustine's"—and probably the oldest in England—is a case in point. Formerly there was a charter of King Ethelbald prefixed to it, which was thought to have settled its date. But the fact is this charter no more belonged to it originally, than what is bound up with it still. Obviously, there are three qualities of parchment, and at least four styles of handwriting in the existing volume. It begins with a preface to the Psalms in Latin. This is written in capitals, which are neither the capitals of the Psalter, nor of the other pieces which precede the Psalter; but *are* the capitals of the prayer following the psalm "extra numerum," or the Goliah Psalm at the

* Catalogued as "Vespasian A." Waterland has remarked upon it at some length, but not to much purpose. Hist. Crit. pp. 93-6.

end of the Psalter. This psalm, again, though in the same capitals as the rest of the Psalter, was not written by the same hand. The author of the catalogue to these MSS. considers the capitals of the Psalter English, and the rest Italian; but there are really three sorts of capitals to be distinguished, not two. The parts of the volume not in capitals are: 1. A short prayer immediately preceding the Psalter. 2. A miscellaneous collection appended to the Psalter, and comprising the " Te Deum," with this heading: " Hymnus matutinus diebus Dominicis;" the Athanasian Creed, with this: " Incipit fides Catholica;" a prayer with this: " Oratio Eugenii Toletani episcopi"—he lived in the seventh century—the rest is anonymous, and includes a confession to God in Latin, with one leaf left blank; and four prayers or addresses to the Cross, with two more leaves left blank. 3. There is a Saxon version interlined over the entire Psalter proper; and over the

"Te Deum" and Athanasian Creed, which is not in capitals either, but is all by the same hand. The parchment on which everything preceding the Psalter, and the psalm "extra numerum" at the end of the Psalter, is written, is of one quality, that of the Psalter another, and that of the appendix another. The Psalter proper, of which the first leaf is unhappily gone, contains, besides the Psalms, the usual canticles from the Old and New Testament; the hymns for morning and evening, by S. Ambrose; and a hymn for Sundays, which if not his, was at any rate well known and much esteemed when Bede wrote. It contains nothing whatever to point to a later date, and must have been all written by the same hand. It is one of the noblest relics of antiquity we possess; and, for all that appears to the contrary, may have been really what it has long been called, "Augustine's Psalter." But the Saxon translation, with which it has been interlined, and the pieces which have been prefixed and appended to it since then, are *mere parasites*, and of different growths; the charter, the preface to the psalms, and the psalm "extra numerum," probably the earliest; the other pieces in capitals preceding the psalms, the next; the prayer before the psalms, the Saxon translations, and the appendix, the last. In the catalogue, the appendix is held to have been penned about the time of the Conquest. I think there can be no doubt of the prayer before the psalms and the Saxon translations being by the same hand.

What is called "Athelstan's Psalter" in the same collection* is a case in point also, but of another description. It has been bound up with a good deal that is extraneous to it, but its parasites are several of them older than itself. There are several qualities of parchment in the existing volume, and several styles of

* Catalogued as Galba A. xviii.

handwriting, all in small characters. A Calendar, in Latin, comes first. This contains a calculation in one place showing it must have been made A.D. 703, which date has accordingly been claimed for the whole volume. This is negatived summarily by what we read p. 28, where "Charles, the most pious Emperor," is recorded to have "departed this life on the ides of February;" his son "Pepin, glorious King, on the ides of June;" and his grandson, "Bernard, most glorious King, on the ides of May," etc. A prayer for their souls follows. Now, the last of them, Bernard, died A.D. 818. It needs but a glance at the parchment and handwriting to see that the Calendar is a perfectly distinct production from the rest. The Latin prayers, which come next, may or may not have been written by the chronicler of the death of Charlemagne and his descendants, and are, doubtless, in the same hand as the prayers which follow the Psalter, but could not have been penned, anyhow, at the same time with the Psalter, or by the same scribe. This remark applies equally to the short abstract of the Book of Psalms, following the last batch of prayers, and still more to the solitary leaf at the end of the volume, containing a Litany in Greek words, but Saxon characters, savouring of the same age with the Calendar.

The Psalter itself embodies much that forms no part of the one called Augustine's: a fact consistent enough with the age which tradition has assigned both. A prayer for the repose of the souls of Charlemagne and his descendants would be perfectly natural in a Prayer Book of King Athelstan, once the fond pet of his grandfather, Alfred, who began life when their memory was still fresh. This, and the prayers preceding and following the Psalter, may have been written, while the Psalter was in his possession, on what had been left blank leaves till then. In the Psalter proper, the Psalms are preceded by a preface, and supplemented by the Psalm " Extra Numerum." The Canticles, in their usual order, come next; then the " Te Deum," without any title; then the " Gloria in Excelsis," designated as " a hymn for Sundays;" the " Lord's Prayer," and the " Creed," word for word as now used; last of all, the Athanasian Creed, designated as " the faith of S. Athanasius of Alexandria"—all in the same hand and on the same parchment. Athelstan came to the crown A.D. 924. It has been already stated that in Psalters confessedly later than the ninth century the Athanasian Creed is no longer found in an appendix, but figures in what may be called the text of the Psalter. Instances of this kind are supplied by the Harleian MS. 2904 in the British Museum, and Douce MS. 127 in the Bodleian Library, whose Litanies, in the same hand as the Athanasian Creed and Psalter, contain the names of Kings Edmund and Ethel-

NOT AN ORIGINAL WORK. 315

bert amongst the martyrs of the former, and one of the many Dominics commemorated in hagiography, from the eleventh century downwards,* amongst the monks of the latter. Other instances that may be consulted in the British Museum are 2 B.V. of the King's Library, which is assigned in the revised catalogue to the tenth century, instead of the ninth; Vitellius E xviii. among the Cotton MSS., and MS. 863 among the Harleian, which proclaim themselves to be of the same age, or rather more than a century later.

In all MS. copies of the Athanasian Creed that I have seen,† it appears in the exact form in which it has come down to us, word for word as it is still printed in Latin: the only variations being in its

---

* Potthast's Bibl. Hist., s. v.

† And this is what the Benedictine Editors of it say: "Latini codices plerique omnes Symbolum exhibent cum perpaucis varietatibus: uno excepto Colbertino antiquissimo, qui non sententiâ, sed verbo tantum tenus multum discrepat ab editis." Op. S. Athan. ii. 716.

title, which are sufficiently explained by its appearing under a false name. The title given to it in the Roman Breviary is "*Symbolum* S. Athanasii." Theodulph, Bishop of Orleans, as we have seen—I might have added Angilbert, Charlemagne's own Secretary*—called it by this in the ninth century. Later, or even then, it was called "*Fides*" more generally: at the same time, be it remembered, "*Creed*" was in those days one of the senses which "Fides" bore. I make these remarks in reference to what has been advanced on each head by Canon Swainson.† As to Greek versions,

---

* Among the Stat. Rub. attributed to him. "In his vero majoribus Litaniis, *post Antiphonas, Psalmos, aliaque id genus*, cantabantur tria Symbola, Apostolorum, Constantinopolitanum, et S. Athanasii: deinde oratio Dominica." Migne's Patrol. xcix. 850.

† Letter to Dean Hook, pp. 41-3, and 66-70. With reference to the last of these, I would ask also whether ancient commentators in general ever cite more of a work than the passages they select from it for comment?

in reference to what Professor Brewer has said,* I never heard of any Greek writer so much as noticing it till it had been described to the Greeks by the envoys of Gregory IX. A.D. 1233, as having been composed by S. Athanasius in Latin.† It began to be canvassed among them from that time, and was, in all probability, first translated into their own tongue by some Latiniser—possibly by John Veccus himself, sixty years later, after he had ceased to be Patriarch, during his long confinement—to be used as a weapon against his countrymen, who, in turn, accommodated it to their own views. Specimens of each sort may be seen at the end of the second volume of the Benedictine Edition of the works of S. Athanasius;‡ but the subject is not worth pursuing any further.

* Athn. Creed Vindicated, pp. 61-2.
† Above, c. iv. p. 257.
‡ The Editors say of Greek versions in general: " Sanè nullum vidimus Græcum hujus Symboli codicem, qui trecentorum sit annorum : nec anti-

It only remains for me to explain how passages, in appearance from the Athanasian Creed, are found again and again in writers anterior to the ninth century. The fact is that, instead of their being citations from it at all, the Athanasian Creed is, on the contrary, from first to last, a veritable mosaic of such passages. How this escaped Waterland, in digesting matter for his ninth chapter, is, perhaps, to be explained from his notion of the Creed having been composed at a time when original writing was the rule, and not the exception. Had he studied the productions of later ages with half as much care, he could not have failed to have seen that there was a long dreary period when original writing was the exception, not the rule. From the

quum alium a quopiam visum fuisse novimus." And further: "Græcæ formulæ ita inter se dissonant, ut a variis interpretibus ex Latino Græcé versas fuisse conspicuum est." Of the four they give, Nos. 2 and 3 are with the " Filioque," and 1 and 4 without it.

seventh to the twelfth century there was no style more popular, or carried to a greater nicety, than the patchwork style: original only so far as concerned the arbitrary shapes into which the pieces were cut, and the seams by which they were joined together.* Every classical scholar knows what Ausonius makes Virgil say—I refer to it merely for illustration—of the liberties taken with the Fathers two centuries or more later, my contention is not, of course, that they were identical, but they were the same in kind. One writer after another made them say what they never meant: and this was done by piecing passages from the earlier and later Fathers together, a bit here and a bit there, without naming them, always detached from their context, sometimes interpolated, often separated from each other by original remarks or comments, till a position was attained agreeable to the

* Above, pp. 70-2.

age or fancies of the compiler, which none of them singly, or none but the latest, would have owned. The few instances which have been indicated already must suffice. S. Isidore died Bishop of Seville A.D. 636, and S. Ildefonse became Archbishop of Toledo twenty years later. One of the works of the former is "On Ecclesiastical Offices;" of the latter "On the Knowledge of Baptism." Both are good specimens of their kind. S. Ildefonse describes his own work as "a congestion" or "agglomeration" which he had made for the good of the Church, and arranged not for propounding novelties of his own unknown till then, but for unfolding the counsels of the ancients to the intelligence, or noting them down for the memory.* How was this carried out in practice? It is quite possible that in the work thus described there are really more quotations than have been verified

* See the end of his Preface.

NOT AN ORIGINAL WORK. 321

as yet; but as yet the authorities there cited seem practically to be confined to these two: S. Isidore, who was, indeed, no more than his contemporary, though his senior; and S. Augustine. His longest and most frequent quotations are from S. Augustine; but when S. Augustine fails him, he goes to S. Isidore; and when both fail him, he inserts statements of his own.* Whether he had read the Expositions of the Creed by Rufinus and

* Starting from § 33, which contains the extract below, § 34, consisting of six lines, is his own; but § 35 is from the middle of c. 1 from S. Aug. de Fide et Symbolo. § 36-7 are his own once more. § 38 begins and ends with his own, but the intermediate is from S. Aug. ibid., c 2. § 39 is from S. Aug. ibid. c. 3-4; but § 40-2 is from S. Aug. Enchir., c. 38-40. Then to § 45 is from S. Aug. de Fide et S. again, § 45 being in part from S. Isid. Etym. vii. 10, and in part his own. § 47 there is a quotation from S. Isid. Eccl. Off. i. 30; otherwise the rest is all his own to § 50. What is said on "the Ascension," etc. in the three next sections is from S. Aug. ibid.; but the seven sections which follow on "the Holy Ghost" are all from S. Isid. Etym. vii. 3, where the Latin view of the Procession is maintained as a dogma.

Y

S. Nicetas for himself, or got at them only through S. Isidore, I leave to others to judge; but I set down a specimen from each to show how the process of dovetailing quotations in those days was carried out, and one writer made to speak for another. The italicised portions are from Rufinus, as now edited in each case; the remainder from S. Nicetas.

S. Isidore, Eccl. Off. ii. 33.	S. Ildefonse, Cogn. Bapt., § 33.
Discessuri itaque, ut dictum est, ad prædicandum, istud unanimitatis et fidei suæ Apostoli indicium posuere.	*Pro solidate itaque initianda fidei bene discessuri ab invicem Apostoli hoc unanimitatis indicium posuerunt.*
Est autem Symbolum per quod agnoscitur Deus, quodque proinde credentes accipiunt, ut noverint qualitèr contra diabolum fidei certamina præparent: in quo quidem pauca sunt verba, sed omnia continentur incrementa. *De totis enim Scripturis hæc breviatim collecta*	Quod Symbolum est signum vel indicium per quod agnoscitur Deus: quod ideò credentes accipiunt ut sciant qualitèr certamen fidei contra diabolum præparent: in quo cùm pauca sint verba, continentur omnia Sacramenta. In quo ideò *ab Apostolis* breviatim

sunt ab Apostolis, ut quoniam plures credentium literas nesciunt, vel qui sciunt per occupationes sæculi Scripturas legere non possunt, hæc corde retinentes habeant sufficientem sibi scientiam salutarem. *Est enim breve fidei verbum ut olim a Prophetâ prædictum:* "*Quoniam verbum breviatum faciet Dominus super terram.*"*

collecta sunt ex omnibus Scripturis, ut quia nulli credentes vel literas nescirent, vel scienter occupati impedimento sæculi Scripturas iis legere non liceret, hoc corde et memoriâ retinentes sufficientem sibi haberent scientiam salutarem."

---

* The passages themselves run thus in R. and N.:

Rufinus, § 2. "Discessuri igitur, ut diximus, ad prædicandum istud unanimitatis et fidei suæ Apostoli indicium possuere." . . . .

Then § 1: "In his verò completur prophetia quæ dicit: verbum enim consummans, et brevians in æquitate quia verbum breviatum faciet Dominus super terram." . . . .

S. Nicetas, § 13. "Retinete semper pactum quod fecistis cum Domino: id est, hoc symbolum quod coram angelis et hominibus confitemini. Pauca quidam sunt verba, sed omnia continent Sacramenta. De totis enim Scripturis hæc brevitatis causâ collecta sunt tanquam gemmæ pretiosæ in unâ coronâ compositæ, ut quoniam plures cre-

The passage cited by them as from Rufinus occurs at the end of the legendary tale tacked to his work which S. Isidore is the first to cite, and may have composed, as I suggested in my first chapter. Let this be denied, and it will not exculpate them anyhow for tampering with S. Nicetas as they have. His beautiful observation is, that "these things were collected from all parts of Scripture, like precious gems, to adorn one crown;" they robbed him of his poetry, and put a word of their own into his mouth which he never uttered: viz., "that they were collected *by the Apostles.*" As it cannot be denied that they have both interpolated S. Nicetas, why should it be thought incredible that one of them should have interpolated Rufinus? Alcuin, or the writer of a work attributed to him, has quoted S. Nicetas no less unfairly. S.

dentium literas nesciunt, vel qui sciunt, per occupationes sæculi Scripturis legere non possunt, habeant sufficientem sibi scientiam salutarem" . .

Nicetas besides explaining the Creed, wrote "on the power of the Holy Ghost:" and in doing so, laid down the doctrine of His Procession in strict harmony with the uninterpolated Creed. Alcuin in his own profession of faith starts with a quotation word for word from S. Nicetas on the first article:[*] but commences the articles relating to the Holy Ghost by defending its interpolation. "And, therefore, not with another, nor a different, but with one and the same faith," he says, "I profess my belief in the Holy Ghost, the Lord and Giver of Life, Who proceedeth from the Father and the Son." He must have known that this had not been hitherto the teaching of the Church, or he would not have apologised for it: though he was, of course, free to maintain it, if it had not been condemned. But he had no business, after this, to make S. Nicetas testify

[*] Confess. Fid. iii. 20. The quotation is from Explan. Symb. § 2.

to all he professed: and transfer what the bishop had said of the statement of the Aquileian Creed on the Trinity to his own.* "This rule of faith the Apostles received from the Lord that they should baptize all believers in the Name of the Father, Son, and Holy Ghost." However, S. Nicetas was not the only writer who was so served.

One of the best known works of Alcuin, as was stated in my first chapter, is one dedicated to Charlemagne on the Trinity. There is nothing in its dedication† that would lead us to infer that it was a compilation, still less a compilation from a single author, as it purports to be a statement of the *Catholic* doctrine of the Trinity. But even contemporaries described it as having been collected from different works of S. Augustine;‡ and

* Confess. Fid. c. 23, and Explan. Symb. § 8.
† M. Migne's Patrol. ci. 11-13.
‡ As Teganus said on sending it to Bishop Hatto: "Ideò istud volumen vobis transmisi, quod sanctus Alcuinus summus scholasticus ex

several of the MSS. containing it exhibit a note to this effect, at the end of the third book.* Further, the whole of the first book, and the three first chapters of the second, came to be circulated in a separate form† as a sermon by S. Augustine, with this title: "De Trinitate et Columba." But the truth is, it is a compilation, and it is not a compilation. S. Augustine seems the only writer quoted in it; and as far as the letter goes, it consists from first to last of passages strung together from him. But the tone throughout is as unlike his as could be conceived.‡ It is positive where he was diffident, dogmatic where he was only speculative, menacing where he was meekness itself. The compiler adopts his language but to

variis libris S. Augustini congregavit in unum." Patrol. ci. 9.

* " Explicit liber iii. de S. Trinitate, quam excerpsit Alcuinus de libris S. Augustini." Ib. 58.

† Serm. xxxviii. "De Tempore:" was its place among his Sermons formerly: but the Benedictines rejected it altogether.

‡ Alcuin, de Trin. i. 16.

express his own thoughts: instantly changing it when it lags behind them. He would have people think they are reading S. Augustine when they are reading his treatise, but he takes care that it shall be but himself who speaks. He wants all his authority, and is ready to accept as much of his sentiment as will bear out his own. Witness the beginning of their respective works. " Should anybody reading me," says the bishop,* " object: 'I understand what is said

---

* De Trin. i. 4, he had said even of the received doctrine of the Trinity: "Sed primum, secundum auctoritatem Scripturarum, sanctarum utrum, ita se fides habeat demonstrandum est." Again, ix. 1., " Quod ergo ad istam quæstionem altinet, credamus Patrem et Filium et Spiritum Sanctum esse unum Deum . . . nec Patrem esse Filium nec Spiritum Sanctum vel Patrem esse vel Filium : sed Trinitatem relatarum adinvicem Personarum, et Unitem æqualis essentui. Hoc autem quæramus intelligere ab Eo Ipso, Quem intelligere volumus, auxilium precantes ut quantum tribuit quod intelligimus explicare tantâ curâ et sollicitudine pietatis cupientes, ut etiam si aliquid aliud pro alio dicimus, nihil tamen indignum dicamus. . .

perfectly, but it is not well said:' let him assert his own opinion if he will, and refute mine if he can. Now, should he do this with truth and charity, and make known the same to me, should I be alive, it would be the greatest benefit that I could reap from my work." And a good deal more to the same effect.

All this was foreign to the genius of the compiler; consequently the opening of his work is drawn from another source. "For those who wish to attain to the true bliss, faith is before all things necessary: according to the teaching of the Apostle, which says: 'Without faith it is impossible to please God.' It is clear, therefore, that nobody can attain to the true bliss except he please God: and that nobody can please God except through faith.... Every rational being, then, on arriving at a suitable age, should learn the Catholic faith." * ... viz. what he is

* Alcuin de Trin. i. 3. What is omitted before the words "every rational being" is taken word

about to lay down as such; dovetailing S. Augustine in the manner already described, and as the following will also show:

1. S. Aug. de Trin. i. 4.

"All the Catholic commentators on the Holy Scriptures of the Old and New Testament who have written on the Trinity in the Godhead before me, that I have read, have concurred in teaching according to the Scriptures, that the Father, Son, and Holy Ghost indicate a divine unity of one and the same substance, equal and inseparable; so that there are not three Gods but one God."

Alcuin de Trin. i 3.

"*All the inspired Scriptures of the Old and New Testament, interpreted in a Catholic sense*, indicate that the Father, Son, and Holy Ghost is one God, of the same substance, of one essence, and inseparable unity in the Godhead."

The opening paragraph was not sweeping enough for the compiler: but as

for word from S. Fulgent, de fide ad Pet. Prol. § 1, which Peter Lombard (Sentent. i. 19. 5.) quotes as a work of S. Aug., as did Theodulph (Patrol.

altered by him, it asserts too much by half.

2. S. Aug. de Trin. v. ii.	Alcuin de Trin. i. 6.
"Accordingly, the Holy Ghost is in some sort the ineffable communion of the Father and the Son: and is therefore, perhaps, so called, because the same designation is applicable to the Father and the Son."	"Accordingly this gift of God, viz., the Holy Ghost, *Who proceeds equally from the Father and the Son*, is in some sort the ineffable communion of the Father and the Son: and is therefore perhaps so called, because the same designation is applicable to the Father and the Son."

Here the compiler has interpolated S. Augustine with a phrase he never used: "Who proceeds *equally* from the Father and the Son." What S. Augustine taught on this head distinctly, was, that the Holy Ghost proceeds "*princi-*

cv. 257-8) *then*. All in the text seems his own; though the idea is the same. The well-known formula of Pope Hormisdas—" Prima salus est regulam rectæ fidei custodire " (Patrol. lxxiii. 393) may have suggested both.

pally" from the Father, and by His gift from the Son too.* But this Alcuin everywhere carefully suppressed. People, therefore, who supposed that in reading Alcuin they were reading S. Augustine, were deceived both ways. Nor was this all by any means. Alcuin, as has been stated, dedicated his work to Charlemagne. Let us see what he said on that occasion. First, he declares his object in writing it to have been, to supply Charlemagne with "a manual" on the faith of the Holy and Undivided Trinity; and this, as he says, not because he deemed any part of it unknown to the superior wisdom of the Emperor, but that he

* *E.g.* xv. 17. "In hac Trinitate non dicitur verbum Dei nisi Filius; nec Donum Dei nisi Spiritus Sanctus; nec de Quo genitum est verbum, et de Quo procedit principalitèr Spiritus Sanctus nisi Deus Pater. Ideo autem additur *principalitèr*, quia et de Filio Spiritus Sanctus procedere reperitur." . . . And again, c. 26: "Filius de Patre natus est: et Spiritus Sanctus de Patre *principalitèr*, et Ipso sine ullo temporis intervallo dante, communitèr de Utroque procedit." . . .

might discharge the office of "Master," as he had been named by some, and convince others who thought it waste of time for the Emperor to carry out his noble intention of learning the rules of the art of logic, which blessed Augustine, in his books on the Trinity, showed *he thought eminently necessary*, by proving that the deepest questions on the Holy Trinity could not be solved without recourse to the subtle distinctions of the categories." . . . Never was a more mischievous gloss put upon one writer by another. S. Augustine never expressed or implied anything of the kind. The portion of his work to which Alcuin refers is the fifth book; and the account given by his Benedictine editors of the contents of this book is as follows: " Coming to those positions of the heretics, which they found not upon Scripture, but their own reasonings, he refutes them," etc. As he had said himself: " Wherefore, that we may begin to reply to the adversaries of our faith concerning those things which are not spoken of as they are thought, nor thought of as they are, among the many things urged commonly by the Arians against the Catholic faith, this they seem to consider one of their strongest points: namely, the distinction which they draw when they say: 'Whatever is said or thought of God, must fall under the head of substance, not of accident.'"* .... And his reply to it, which he developes at great length, and presses home with overwhelming force, is that some things are said of the Godhead relatively: that is, in describing the relations of the Divine Persons composing It to Each Other, or to the creation. In this way he meets them on their own ground, and annihilates them with their own weapons; but it is refutation all through: it was never intended to be constructive. Alcuin simply perverted it in making it the basis of a dogmatic

* v. 2.

system; and in devoting a chapter to the elucidation of the categories in a formal exposition of the Catholic faith of the Trinity, as though the one could and ought to be explained by the other, he put a fatal gloss upon S. Augustine which has stuck to him ever since, and impregnated the springs of dogmatic theology with false principles on the highest of all subjects in the West ever since, under cover of his name. It has been said in praise of the schoolmen in general that they Christianised Aristotle; it is undeniable that on one point at least, and that a cardinal one, they rationalised Christianity.*

"All which things," says Alcuin, in conclusion, "devoutly considering with myself, I have chosen the time of the large gathering of the priests of God, and preachers of Christendom assembled at your command, for laying before your

* "Difficulties of the Day, and how to meet them," pp. 55-7, where examples are given.

most excellent majesty such a mass of resources, as I believe will not prove inefficacious, in the matter of the Catholic faith; supposing at least that God, Who gave me the will to speak, has, as I trust he has of His mercy, enlightened my heart with the spirit of grace to the discernment of the truth. Wherefore, in answer to the prayers of the whole body of faithful people, it is much to be desired, that your empire may be extended with all glory: to *the end that the Catholic faith*, which alone quickens the human race, which alone sanctifies it, may *be imprinted in one confession on the hearts of all;* so that by the gracious gift of the Almighty, the same unity both of holy peace and perfect love may govern and protect all men everywhere."

Alcuin had his wish fulfilled to the letter; in point of fact he contributed as much as anybody to its fulfilment. The empire of Charlemagne *was* extended, as he had prayed, in process of time, *with all glory;* for it established a hold on the mind of Europe, which it maintains to this day, by employing as a means, what he had proposed as its end. "The large gathering" to which he refers, was the Synod of Aix, A.D. 802, where Paulinus and he received their crowns; where his own work on the Trinity received the imperial *imprimatur*, and all the deference due to a standard authority from that time forth; and where all ecclesiastics of the empire were required "to learn the Catholic faith of S. Athanasius," then published for the first time. "*The Catholic faith*, which alone quickens, which alone sanctifies the human race, *will be soon imprinted in one confession on the hearts of all* by these means," argued the correspondent of Alcuin, and the framer of this capitulary; "nor will there be wanting a corner-stone to my empire, when it has become law. Augustine epitomised shall be the text-book of my theologians;

Athanasius epitomised a rule of faith for my clergy." He had, probably, with his own hand, given the finishing stroke to both before they were published. He was well aware of the principles on which both were compiled. If there was any difference between them it was confined to details, which so far imparted a touch of originality to each. The work of Alcuin was compiled virtually from one writing of one writer; that of Paulinus from many writings of many writers; still all of the same school. The work of Alcuin issued forth in his own name; but it consisted almost entirely of passages from S. Augustine, and from him alone. The work of Paulinus passed for a composition of S. Athanasius; but, in reality, there was not a word from first to last in it quoted from him. In the work of Alcuin the pieces forming the patchwork were cut large; in that of Paulinus they were cut small.

Waterland, as has been stated already,

collected a number of parallel passages, or, more strictly, morsels from S. Augustine, out of which he might, if he had tried, have manufactured another Athanasian Creed with ease; but the idea never seems to have struck him, that it had really been compiled in this way. His object in throwing them together, as he tells us, had been "to show that the Creed contained nothing but what had been asserted in as full and express words, as any words of the Creed are, by church writers before A.D. 430."* But in the first place, strange to say, there is but one parallel of his whole list drawn from any church writer but one, viz. S. Augustine; and next, Waterland should have remembered, to revert to the extreme case before touched upon, that it was precisely *by quoting Virgil word for word*, that Ausonius perverted him. Neither Waterland's parallels from S. Augustine, nor even Autelmi's parallels from S. Vincen-

* Crit. Hist. c. ix. p. 226.

tius of Lerins, are to the point, till it has first been shown, that *they mean in their own context* all that they are adduced to support in the Creed. The truest parallels to it are not found till the speculations of S. Augustine had been converted into positive dogma; his meaning assumed or glossed upon, where it had not been explicit; and innumerable tracts and sermons circulated as his which a later age had produced. Paulinus had doubtless a common-place book, in which he wrote down extracts from whatever came in his way that struck him most, ranging them under various heads, in order to have them ready for use at any moment, as occasion required. If he drew from originals, the works of which he may be supposed to have made most use would be that of S. Augustine on the Trinity, besides his smaller treatises on the Creed, on Faith, Hope, and Charity, and so forth; the Commonitorium of S. Vincentius; Vigilius of Thapsus on the Trinity; S.

Fulgentius on the Trinity, and on the Faith to Peter the Deacon. I know of no one work that more resembles the Athanasian Creed in style and in tone than this; and this, somehow or other, got placed among the works of S. Augustine. Lastly, the work on Etymologies by S. Isidore. Or, again, he may have drawn from a later class of writings that were drawn from these. One of the sermons on the Creed formerly given to S. Augustine, for instance, began thus:

"I admonish and entreat you, dearly beloved brethren, that whosoever will be saved, learn, hold firmly, and maintain inviolate the right and Catholic faith. So then ought everybody to see, that he believe the Father, that he believe the Son, that he believe the Holy Ghost. The Father God, the Son God, and the Holy Ghost God: nevertheless not three Gods, but one God. Such as the Father, such the Son, and such the Holy Ghost. At the same time let every faithful soul believe that the Son is equal to the Father as touching His Godhead, and inferior to the Father as touching His Manhood of the flesh which He took of ours. And the Holy Ghost proceeding from Both."*

Most of the remainder is really taken from S. Augustine; but the opening sentence is unique; and to this, it can hardly be doubted, the author of the Creed was indebted for his first verse.

King Reccared, in conjunction with it, may have suggested his next: "Should any be unwilling to believe this our right and holy confession, may they be made to feel the wrath of God with everlasting anathema.†

Passing by "The Rule of Faith," of unknown authorship and uncertain date, then extant in Spain, as having been

---

* S. Aug. Op. v. Append. Serm. ccxliv. Ed. Migne. It is assigned by the Benedictines to S. Cæsarius of Arles, but cannot be earlier than the seventh century.

† Mansi, ix, 980.

given already,* the fourth Synod of Toledo probably suggested the two verses which follow, and several on the Incarnation:

"Believing a Trinity in the distinction of Persons, and preaching an Unity in the Godhead, we neither confound the Persons nor divide the Substance." .... Then of our Lord: "having the properties of two Natures in one Person, ... enduring passion and death for our salvation. ...... He descended into hell, ... and shall come again to judge both the living and the dead: who will receive from Him, some, for their deserts of righteousness, eternal life; others, for their sins, the sentence of eternal punishment. This is the faith of the Catholic Church; this confession we keep and hold; this anybody, by preserving most firmly, will have everlasting salvation."†

* Above, p. 194-6.
† C. 1, Ibid. x. 616.

The eleventh Synod of Toledo may well have suggested others:

" For should we be asked of each of the Persons, we must of necessity confess Him God. So the Father by Himself is called God, the Son God, the Holy Ghost God: yet not three Gods, but one God. So also the Father by Himself is called Almighty, the Son Almighty, and the Holy Ghost Almighty: yet not three Almighties, but one Almighty. . . . Each Person, therefore, by Himself, is believed and confessed full God, and the whole Three Persons one God. One, undivided and equal Divinity, power, and majesty They have, which is not smaller in Each, nor larger in all Three: for neither has Each less, when called by Himself God, nor all Three more, when together called God. . . These Three, then, are One: that is, in Nature, but not in Person; still neither as Persons are They to be considered separable. Forasmuch as neither may

One be believed to have existed before or after Another, nor One to have wrought a work at any time without Another." ...

A century later the Elipandian or Adoptionist controversy brought the doctrine of the Incarnation, and all the former errors by which it had been assailed, into special prominence. Accordingly, such passages as these are of frequent occurrence:

"The Father alone is of none, but of Himself.

The Son is of the Father, not of Himself.

The Holy Ghost is of the Father and the Son, not of Himself.* . . . . .

Wherefore, the Son alone was made Man: in the Unity, not of Nature, but of Person.† . . . . Such, then, was that assumption, which made God Man, and Man God: and of Both One Christ.‡ . . .

---

* Eter. et Beat. ad Elip. 1-19 in Migne's Patrol. xcvi. 905.
† Ibid. ii. 74, p. 1016. ‡ Ibid. i. 127, p. 973.

For as the soul and body, being of a different substance, is one man, so God and Man, being of a different substance, is one Christ.* . . . Thus much on the Trinity. Now on the grace by which we are redeemed, according to the teaching of our Mother the Church. Forasmuch as both to believe rightly, and think truly, respecting the Mediator of God and Man, true and perfect Man, our Lord and Saviour Jesus Christ belongs, undoubtedly, to everlasting salvation.† . . . Whosoever shall deviate from the true faith, shall not have the grace of salvation."‡ . . .

These specimens must suffice. From such materials the Creed was, undoubtedly, put together verse by verse; nor is it at all necessary to suppose that it was put together in bad faith. But, in the first place, we have to deal with

* Eter. et Beat. ii. 60, p. 1011.
† Alcuin, Conf. Fid. iii. 2.
‡ Eter. et Beat. i. 95, p. 953.

the Creed as it was published: and it was published as a work of S. Athanasius, when, literally, there was not a verse in it that had been culled from him. And, literally, the first use to which it was turned was to assail the Creed, which was his parting bequest to the Church, for such the Niceno-Constantinopolitan Creed really was.* These are facts which cannot be explained away, whatever may be thought of its intrinsic merits. But, again, let it be supposed to be a correct exponent of the mind of S. Augustine, from whom so much of it is undoubtedly borrowed. What then? Professing to be "the Catholic faith," it represents the mind of a single Father! Is this a contradiction in terms or not, to begin with? And next, are there no points of doctrine on which S. Augustine has not been followed? But, further, *is it* a faithful exponent of his mind? Certainly not: so far as it converts into

* Above, p. 207, note.

dogma what had been speculation with him, appeals to logic instead of Scripture, and menaces any with perdition who will not accept terms which he long hesitated about using at all, and at last only justified *in controversial works*, and from the sheer necessities of the case even then.* Let it have been compiled—*published it cannot have been*—in ever so good faith, it no more represents the mind of S. Augustine than of S. Athanasius, but is a gloss upon both. The spirit it represents is that of the African Church in the fifth and sixth centuries; of the Spanish Church in the seventh—both overrun then by barbarians; and of the divines of Charlemagne in the eighth

* Above, p. 214, note, I continue the quotation. He is speaking of "Substance" and "Person" as distinguished from each other. "Quid igitur restat nisi ut fateamur *loquendi necessitate* posita hæc vocabula, cum *opus esset copiosâ disputatione* adversum insidias vel errores hæreticorum?" De Trin. vii. 5.

and ninth centuries above all, whose work it was: and with this spirit it has been the means of indoctrinating Latin Christendom everywhere for one thousand years at what may be called the point of the sword. It is perfectly true, as I have seen alleged somewhere, that the word " anathema" never occurs in it: there might have been just the shadow of a doubt as to what that word meant, and consequently some ground for hope, if it had *only said*, " Let him be anathema."* It affirms, therefore, categorically, and without reserve, of all that it has laid down *en masse*, that *it* " is the

---

* The popular meaning attached to this word is one thing, its strict meaning another. It now and then occurs in no bad sense at all, but as a simple offering to God. And it is on this sense that all that it ever means is founded. It is a thing " set apart " or " separated " to God, to do what He will with, and in the worst of cases, there is always a chance that God may pardon what man condemns, or bless where man has cursed. See Suicer's Thesaur, s. v.

Catholic faith, which, except a man believe faithfully, he *cannot*, or *will not be able to* be saved." *Salvus esse non poterit*, as it is in the Latin.

CHAPTER VI.

CONCLUDING REMARKS.

THAT Charlemagne settled both creeds and dogma for the West, and established a breach between Eastern and Western Christendom on dogmatic grounds, by means of his general capitulary directing the "Catholic Faith" of S. Athanasius and the "Apostles' Creed" to be learnt by the clergy throughout his empire, A.D. 802, is a simple fact. Aquileia supplied him with the materials he wanted: he accommodated them to his own purposes and in his own way. From Aquileia came the legend of the Western Creed having been composed by the Apostles; from Aquileia the article, which in primitive times it wanted, of the descent of our Lord into hell; from Aquileia, most probably, the Latin version of the Niceno-Constantinopolitan Creed used by King Reccared in Spain, and interpolated with the "Filioque" clause;* from Aquileia, most certainly, that "appraisement of the Catholic faith,"† which has been learnt so long as the Athanasian Creed. There was a sinister look about them all. The names of the two Creeds were fictitious: the "descent into hell" and the "Filioque" clause had never, till recently, stood in any orthodox Creed, and as yet both were unauthorised. Charlemagne legitimatised them all in appropriating them to his own ends. From the time that

* Above, p. 57-70. To which add the fact that S. Isidore himself has not a word about the Fifth Council in any of his extant works. He passes it over notably Etym. vi. 16, and in the Collection of Canons ascribed to him, where a later hand has inserted mention of the Sixth Council. It is not named in the Pseudo-Isidorian Collection. See Migne's Patrol. lxxxiv. 138. S. Isidore's fullest comments on the descent into hell are in his treatise "De Fid. Cath.," Lib. ii. c. 50-54.

† Above, p. 228.

the Western Creed, *as it stood then*, was ordered to be learnt as the " Creed of the Apostles ;" and the work of Paulinus as the " Catholic Faith of S. Athanasius," by the whole empire: no western ever doubted about the one being an inspired composition in its existing form, or the other being its proper exponent. The orthodoxy of the Niceno-Constantinopolitan Creed itself was impeached—and Charlemagne headed the opposition in impeaching it—where it differed from these ; till at length there was no hesitation in pronouncing its teaching on one point at least complete. The " Filioque" clause, which had been added to it in Spain, had been added rightly, and those who refused to admit it were heretics. As it was expressed in the " Faith of S. Athanasius," it ought to have been expressed, had it not been surreptitiously cancelled? in the Creed of Nicæa and Constantinople : said the West, two centuries later. The shortcomings of the Niceno-

Constantinopolitan Creed were made patent on another point, as time went on; though this was not avowed all at once. "The descent of our Lord into hell," was not this an article of faith in the Apostles' Creed, and in the Creed of S. Athanasius alike? Should it not, therefore, be taught as such? As such it was accordingly taught in the West; but in process of time, the mediæval doctrine of purgatory was evolved from it, and is to this day bound up with it, as the Catechism of the Council of Trent attests.* When the representatives of the Eastern and Western Churches assembled at the Council of Florence in the fifteenth century to consider the points on which they differed, the doctrines which had flowed from the irregular admission of the "Filioque" clause in one Creed, and of

* Part I. Art. v. § 5. "Præterea est purgatorius ignis . . . . Ac de hujus quidem doctrinæ veritate . . . . eo diligentius et sæpius parocho disserendum erit, quod in ea tempora incidimus, quibus homines sanam doctrinam non sustinent."

"the descent into hell" in the other, were literally found to be the only two points of any moment, and were therefore the only two points discussed at any length, on which the teaching of the West and the East differed. Both had been first declared *necessary to salvation* in the Athanasian Creed: since its publication the East and West have never been able to agree about them; accordingly, the very purpose which Charlemagne had in publishing it survives to this day. But there were still graver effects produced by its publication, whether he foresaw them or not, on which a few words must be said.

There is evidence that Charlemagne, in ordering the "Faith of S. Athanasius" and the "Creed of the Apostles" to be learnt by his clergy *meant* to substitute the "Faith of S. Athanasius" for the Nicene. Was it that he was fully conscious of the antagonism that exists between them, and contemplated the full effects of his ordinance on the minds of men, on thought and action in the remote future? Yet the connection between cause and effect must have been obvious enough to smaller minds than his even then. The immemorial boast of the Nicene Creed was its Scriptural language: having been confined to this on the principle that it alone is inspired, and therefore certain to express what God has revealed: on the principle that belief in God, to which this Creed was limited originally, should be professed in His own words. One word had, indeed, after the fullest deliberation, been admitted there, which was not of this character, but it stood alone, and was such an exception as proved the rule. A rule relaxed advisedly that the Founder of the Christian religion might be declared God in the strictest sense possible could admit of no further exception. Its inviolableness was again illustrated when the Creed was enlarged. Belief in the Holy Ghost, though professed with much greater fulness than before, was limited to what

Revelation says of Him in express terms. As the remaining Articles had not occurred at all in the original Creed, this rule was not applicable to them directly: and any deviation from it in their case was more than counterbalanced by the speedy application of another rule to the entire Creed in its enlarged form, viz. that of finality. It was, in fact, no sooner promulgated in this shape than it was declared final. Its teaching on the Trinity was pronounced perfection, as it stood then; the smallest addition to it on any subject was interdicted under pains and penalties, and it was ordered to stand as it was stereotyped for public use to the exclusion of all other creeds in future. The mind of the Church in insisting upon these two rules is self-evident. By the first the action of the reason is excluded peremptorily from the domain of faith: and faith itself is limited, in describing each mystery, to language which the Holy Ghost had specially set apart for that purpose. By the second, new Articles of Faith, as well as new Professions of Faith for public use, were forbidden. The sum of all doctrine necessary to salvation having been expressed in the existing Creed—the decree said virtually—Be it enacted that no believer shall in future be required to profess more. Simultaneously with this last rule, the anathema which had been appended to this Creed in its original state was tacitly dropped, as being no longer necessary.

Everybody must admit the marked contradiction to both these rules in the Athanasian Creed. In opposition to the first, it invites reason to assist in mapping out the province of faith, utilizes its deductions without scruple in the construction of dogma: invoking the laws of dialectics where Scripture is silent in expounding mysteries, and terms of philosophy where Scriptural terms will not express its own subtleties to the full. In opposition to the second, it declares all that it contains necessary to salvation, whether found in the Creed of the Church or not : some of them being points which must have been omitted from the Creed of the Church by design.*

Nothing can be clearer than the antagonism that exists between them : so that if the principles on which the Church's Creed was constructed were right, the principles on which the Athanasian Creed was constructed were wrong ; so that the latter is false in principle, as well as in name; and false—not on my showing, nor on the showing of any single individual or collection of individuals, ancient or modern, but false on the showing of all the General Councils by whom the Church's Creed was framed and confirmed, and whose authoritative teaching it was deliberately published under a lying

* I instance the expression borrowed from the Aquileian Creed, which involves a conflict with science : that men will rise with "*their own bodies.*" Which ? those they were born with, had in mature age, or died with ?

name, and for political ends, to undermine.

Will it be asked what the effects of its publication have been? The answer is written in history; it meets us in broad daylight; it is patent to angels and men. The division which its publication was intended to promote has become chronic even to the lines of thought. There is one part of the Church where the faith of the true S. Athanasius continues to be the unalloyed standard of doctrine to this day; where the authority of the Church's Creed in the exact form in which it was promulgated is as undisputed as it ever was, and new doctrines as well as new creeds are unknown—where throughout all its vicissitudes, amounting at times almost to annihilation, the provinces of reason and faith have been kept jealously distinct, and where consequently there is not, nor has ever been any standing for rationalism. And in this part, which men have ridiculed as crystallised and hope-

CONCLUDING REMARKS. 361

lessly stagnant till now, there are signs of taking root downwards, and bearing fruit upwards as for a second spring, which none can dispute. Contrariwise, there is another part of the Church which is "ever learning, and never able to come to the knowledge of the truth:" which has multiplied its creeds, till their name is "Legion;" which has added to its creeds, till each one of them is a "Macrostyche:" a farrago of religion, morals, politics, metaphysics, church order, church discipline, and what not—and still its list of dogmas is far from completed—and this, as we have been told of late years, in virtue of its office of developing doctrine— what if its true name should be that of *rationalising the faith?* And in this part all the old land-marks of the Church have been gradually swept away in favour of a despotism, on which everything accordingly, from the least to the greatest, depends, and whose last expedient for supporting itself has been to declare that do what it will it cannot do wrong. This is that part of the Church, whose teachers have been imbibing their principles, Sunday after Sunday for one thousand years, from the faith of the false S. Athanasius; and the effect has been that they have authorised reason to legislate in matters of faith; thought of nothing so much as the *logic* of their conclusions; and claimed as matters of faith every subject worth claiming of which the reason takes cognisance. It is self-evident that in a system like this there can be no limit to dogma; it is also self-evident that the security for each new dogma lies in its having been drawn logically from others previously received. Thus the Vatican decrees are the logical consequence of the teaching of the schools—so much was acknowledged by their promoters—and it was realized in framing them, that they must stand or fall together. But the logical connection between the teaching of the schools and the Athanasian

Creed is no less certain; and their historical connection is indisputable. From which it also follows that Charlemagne endowed the Latin Church with many more things, and things of much greater importance than merely broad lands. The Latin Church as a system—as the Established Church of Europe, to call things by their right names—is a tree that has grown out of his loins. He endowed it with its theology, when he put into the hands of his clergy the " Faith" of the pseudo-Athanasius to be learnt, and the work of Alcuin on the Trinity to be studied by them at the Synod of Aix, A.D. 802; he endowed it with its discipline at the Synod of Aix, A.D. 816, presided over by his son and successor, of which Dean Milman says no less eloquently than justly:*

The four great acts of this Council were among the boldest and most comprehensive ever submitted to a great national assembly. The Emperor

---

* Lat. Christ. III. 117.

was still in theory the sole legislator; not only were the secret suggestions, but the initiatory motives from the supreme power. It might seem that in the three acts which regarded the hierarchy the Emperor legislated for the Church; but it was in truth the Church legislating for herself through the Emperor. It was Teutonised Latin Christianity organising the whole Transalpine Church, with no regard of the Western Pontiff. It was *the completion, ratification, extension of Charlemagne's scheme*—a scheme by its want of success or universality still awaiting its consummation. The vast reforms comprehended at once the whole clergy and the monasteries. *All these laws are enacted by the Emperor in Council for the whole empire—almost tantamount to Latin Christendom—of approbation, ratification, confirmation by the Pope, not one word.*

It has indeed been pretended that Paulinus sat at the first of these synods as legate of the Pope. I do not see what difference it need make to the argument if he did. Two bishops are said to have represented the Pope at Frankfort, where the Second Nicene Council was formally condemned, which they were aware his Holiness had as formally confirmed.[*]

[*] "Christendom's Divisions," ii. 394.

And again, what greater liberties were ever taken with any Pope than were taken by these Caroline divines with Eugenius II. in dictating to him where his duty lay, in reflecting upon the acts of his predecessors, at the celebrated Synod of Paris against images, A.D. 825, which the Pope had no alternative but to accept in silence?*

No! strange to say the really noble part played by some Popes then, is precisely what Rome is most anxious to forget, and to hide now. There were some Popes who saw through the revolutionary designs of Charlemagne, and who resisted the mischief which he was bent upon perpetrating to the utmost of their ability. But the letter of Adrian I. in defence of the Seventh Council and its uninterpolated creed, never saw daylight with the goodwill of Rome, and would

* See the amazement expressed on all this by Baronius: A.D. 824, n. 31-3, and A.D. 825, n. 4, etc.

have been disavowed if it could. The silver tablets of Leo III. on which the uninterpolated creed was engraved, are not among the relics which Rome has preserved. And as for the act of John VIII. in fraternising with Photius, and in summoning S. Methodius, the Apostle of the Sclavonians, to Rome to ask him whether he accepted and used the creed as it had been promulgated by the six first councils and received by Rome,* it procured for him, even while he lived, the scandalous *sobriquet* of Pope Joan, or the female Pope.†

Why would Rome bury the acts of these Popes if she could? Simply for this reason: that, in process of time, when policy dictated, and opportunity offered, she accepted both the doctrine and discipline of Charlemagne as her

* See his own letter to Count Sventopulcher. Ep. 293, in Migne's Patrol. cxxvi. 905, or Baron. A.D. 880, n. 16.

† " Christendom's Divisions," ii. 413.

own, turned her back upon pure, genuine antiquity from thenceforth, and by so doing, in turn, *Latinised the Teuton.* The Apostles' Creed, the Athanasian Creed, she accepted their titles, and bade her clergy recite both as such at the times fixed by Charlemagne.

She accepted the rules he had laid down for Church discipline; she discarded the uninterpolated creed from her Baptismal Office, and commenced using that of the Apostles instead; she introduced the interpolated Creed into her liturgy. The teaching of the false Athanasius and of Alcuin she declared orthodox in opposition to that of the true Athanasius, and to those who persisted in adhering to his faith and that of councils. When shall we have got to the end of her mendaciousness? Teacher of Christendom she claims to be—

"The earth, that in her genial breast
Finds for the down a kindly nest,
When wafted by the warm south-west,
It floats at pleasure:"

is a graphic illustration of the kindly welcome given to fictions in hers! The fiction of the Apostles' Creed was inculcated by her as gospel, as long as anything could be got out of it to her advantage. When this was exploded, she was equally pleased to fall back upon the idea, too hastily propounded by critics, that the Creed so called was really the Roman. It has turned out to be no more the Roman than the Greek.* The Easterns had their creed; the Westerns, including Western Africa, theirs; and Rome hers, which remained stationary, while the rest grew. The Eastern, in process of time, grew to be the Niceno-Constantinopolitan, or the Creed of the Church; the Western to be named after the Apostles; the Roman only to become obsolete even at Rome as a profession. Her candidates for baptism are still examined in it by word of mouth in the form of question and answer; but as a

* Above, c. ii. It is given at length, p. 130.

profession it was exchanged, at first, in obedience to law, for that of the Church; afterwards, from motives of policy, for that of the West. Neither of them had been indebted for a single article they contained to Rome. Both were original and independent compositions, as far as she was concerned. She accepted both without making alterations in either. Her own creed, on the contrary, was enlarged from them.* After this, it would be superfluous to inquire what the teaching office of Rome was when creeds were formed; for there is not, and never has been, a creed in use which the Church owes to her.

Subsequently to her adoption of the Caroline system, she endeavoured to take credit to herself for the creed that underlies it. "The holy Athanasius," she would have the Greeks believe, "had composed it when an exile in the West,"†

---

* Above, pp. 164-7.
† Above, pp. 255-6.

to do honour to Pope Julius whose guest he was. The legend was of course dictated by a consciousness of the secret sources of her own inspiration. The conquest of Constantinople by the Latins had enboldened her to claim, amongst other things which she had never claimed before, to define doctrine. This brings me to the first of what I shall call papal creeds — from their cardinal profession being belief in the Pope—of which the best known to us is that of Pius IV. Down to the ninth century, the utmost claimed by the Popes themselves on behalf of their see had been that, "*as matter of fact, it*," not they, "had never swerved from the faith.*" Pope Adrian had to lay stress on this distinction to get

* Adrian II.'s formula, slightly varied from that of Hormisdas, at the council condemning Photius, A.D. 869. The words 'are, " Et quia non potest D. N. I. C. prætermitti sententia dicentis : ' Tu es Petrus," etc. hæc quæ dicta sunt *rerum probantur effectibus*, quia in sede Apostolicâ immaculata est semper servata religio."

his assertion allowed even so: for as yet everybody remembered, and nobody was as yet audacious enough to deny, the condemnation of Honorius for heresy. Besides, history then deposed to another fact equally pertinent, and doubly patent, till fiction had obscured it, as regards Rome, viz. that it was one thing to *keep* creeds, and another to *make* them. But times were changed when Clement IV. composed his Creed.* He therefore argued, with all the *pseudos*† to back him, "that the Roman Church, as it was credited above all others with having upheld the faith, so it ought, when any questions are raised on doctrine, to define them." And this, after the lapse of six centuries, Pius IX. has capped at last by declaring that he who defines doctrine is infallible.

Such have been the effects of inviting reason to dogmatise in matters of faith,

---

* See this Creed epitomised, in " Christendom's Divisions," ii. 362-3.

† *I.e.* Decretals, donations, legends, etc.

and of empowering logic to heap conclusions one upon another, rigidly mindful of their syllogistic consistency, but in utter indifference to their conformity with objective truth of whatever kind. Hence the dictatorial, inflated, menacing, unreal character which has earned for the teaching of the schools so much contempt; hence the "peremptory, stern, resolute, overbearing, and relentless" mould, the reverse of Christian, attaching to the Church in which it is still upheld. Reason is always exacting and imperious where she reigns unchecked; and she will make use of the imagination to weave fictions for her on any subject where facts are not up to her mark, or else conflict with her axioms. Previously to the publication of the " Novum Organon" of Lord Bacon, it was heresy to impeach the least of the physical nostrums she had derived from her great oracle, Aristotle. And when in our own days the Vatican decrees were published in defiance of history, they were defended on the ground that the appeal to history was treason.

In the same breath a slur was designedly cast upon the memories of De Marca, Bossuet, Mabillon, Montfaucon, Martene, Calmet, Simon, Launoi, Thomassin, Morin, Tillemont, Baluze, Du Pin, and a host of other ornaments of the Gallican Church who had, throughout the whole range of ecclesiastical literature, done so much to clear away the rubbish of ages, to discriminate between truth and falsehood—between primitive truth and medieval fiction—and set truth upon its pedestal once more: and whom, in sacrificing to " the insolent and aggressive faction" as she did recently, France parted with infinitely more glory than she gained at Inkermann or Solferino.

But history, like physical science, is certain to triumph at last: and sooner or later the logic of reason will have to bow low in the dust again before the logic of facts.

The detection of forgeries, will go on till "there is nothing hid that shall not be known:" and all who have been *parties* to "the mystery of iniquity" that has been working among us so long, exposed to public gaze. Then, and not till then, will Christianity be disenchanted of the Spirit of Evil that has for such ages divided her professing members—then, and not till then, will Rome learn to distinguish between what she has inherited from Peter, and what from Charlemagne. And then, lastly, by the combined action of the Greek and Teuton, and all who take part with them, the glorious old religion of the past—so loyally preserved by the former — will live again in adapting itself to the multifarious demands of the times in which we live; when the flame of faith will burn all the brighter from having been purified from the dross of human supports, and the blessings of free thought—by which is *not* meant licence—and of free government—by which is *not* meant anarchy—be secured to the lowest as well as the highest, as well in Church as in State.

S. *Andrew's Day*, 1871.

London: Swift & Co., King Street, Regent Street, W.

Canon 33. C. of Frankfort 794. "Ut fides catholica sanctæ Trinitatis, et oratio dominica, atque symbolum fidei omnibus prædicetur et tradatur." cf. p. 235. Labbe VIII. 105.

Bp Denebert of Worcester in a profession of faith 798 appeals to & quotes the Athanasian creed; & he cites verbatim 9 verses. see Wilk. Concilia. p. iii. 526.

Alcuin +804. speaks of it as made "by the blessed Athanasius himself" the most reverend Bp of the city of Alexandria & received in the universal Church." Migne. cl. p. 71.

The document of Paulinus adopted at Frankfort corresponds to that referred to above p. 226, & is called a libellus. Labbe VIII. 66

WORKS

PUBLISHED BY

J. T. HAYES, LYALL PLACE, EATON SQUARE;

AND

4, HENRIETTA STREET, COVENT GARDEN.

BY REV. W. J. E. BENNETT.

THE "MISSION" SERMONS AT S. PAUL'S, KNIGHTSBRIDGE, in 1869. By Rev. W. J. E. BENNETT, Froome-Selwood. 7s. 6d.; by post, 8s.

A PLEA FOR TOLERATION IN THE CHURCH OF ENGLAND. By W. J. E. BENNETT. Fourth and Cheap Edition. 1s.; by post, 1s. 1d.

OBEDIENCE TO THE LESSER, (The State); DISOBEDIENCE TO THE GREATER, (The Church). By W. J. E. BENNETT. 6d.; by post, 7d.

AGAINST STATE INTERFERENCE IN MATTERS SPIRITUAL: A Reprint from a work entitled "*Remains of Richard Hurrell Froude.*" Preface by W. J. E. BENNETT. 2s.; by post, 2s. 2d.

THE CHURCH'S BROKEN UNITY. Edited by W. J. E. BENNETT, Froome-Selwood. Vol. I., PRESBYTERIANISM AND IRVINGISM. Vol. II., ANABAPTISM, INDEPENDENCY, AND QUAKERS. Vol. III., ON METHODISM, AND THE SWEDENBORGIANS. Each of the first Three Volumes 3s. 6d.; by post, 3s. 10d. Vols. IV. and V., ON ROMANISM. Each, 4s. 6d.; by post, 4s. 10d.

BY REV. DR. LEE.

THE VALIDITY OF THE HOLY ORDERS OF THE CHURCH OF ENGLAND, Maintained and Vindicated both Theologically and Historically; with Foot-Notes, Tables of Consecrations and Appendices. By the Rev. FREDERICK GEORGE LEE, D.C.L., All Saints', Lambeth. Dedicated to the Archbishop of Canterbury. 8vo., 572 pages. 16s.; by post, 17s.

SERMONS, PAROCHIAL AND OCCASIONAL. By Rev. F. G. LEE, D.C.L. 10s. 6d.; by post, 11s.

BY E. S. FFOULKES, B.D.

DIFFICULTIES OF THE DAY, AND HOW TO MEET THEM. Eight Sermons at S. Augustine's, Queen's Gate. By Rev. EDMUND S. FFOULKES, B.D. 3s. 6d.; by post, 3s. 10d.

THE CHURCH'S CREED; THE ROMAN INDEX. In one vol. Cloth, 4s.; by post, 4s. 3d.

Or, separately, as under:—

THE CHURCH'S CREED OR THE CROWN'S CREED? By EDMUND S. FFOULKES, B.D. Sixteenth Thousand. 1s. 6d.; by post, 1s. 7d.

THE ROMAN INDEX AND ITS LATE PROCEEDINGS. By E. S. FFOULKES, B.D. Sixth Thousand. 1s. 6d.; by post, 1s. 8d.

IS THE WESTERN CHURCH UNDER ANATHEMA? A Problem for the Ecumenical Council. By E. S. FFOULKES, B.D. Third Thousand. 1s.; by post, 1s. 1d.

LITURGICAL, &c.

THE NIGHT HOURS OF THE CHURCH: being the Matin Office. Vol. I. From Advent to Trinity. Vol. II. Trinity-tide. Partly arranged by the late Rev. Dr. NEALE, and completed by the Members of S. Margaret's, East Grinsted. (*Vol. III. is in the Press.*)

THE LITURGICAL "REASON WHY:" Being a Series of Papers on the Principles of the Book of Common Prayer. By Rev. A. WILLIAMS, Culmington, Salop; Author of "Home Sermons," &c. 4s.; by post, 4s. 3d.

THE RITUAL "REASON WHY:" Being 450 Ritual Explanations. By C. WALKER, Author of "Liturgy of the Church of Sarum," &c. 4s.; by post, 4s. 4d.

PLAIN WORDS ON THE PSALMS: As translated in the Book of Common Prayer. By MARY E. SIMPSON, Author of "Ploughing and Sowing," &c. With Commendation by the Rev. WALSHAM HOW, M.A., Whittington, Salop. 6s.; by post, 6s. 6d.

THE SERVICES OF THE CHURCH: According to the Use of the Illustrious Church of Sarum. Edited by CHARLES WALKER, Author of "The Liturgy of Church of Sarum," "The Ritual Reason Why," &c. 4s.; by post, 4s. 3d. In Morocco, 6s. 6d. to 12s. 6d.

NOTITIA LITURGICA; Containing Plain Directions for a Low and a High Celebration; Matins and Evensong; Holy Baptism, Confirmation, Holy Matrimony, and Churching of Women; Visitation of the Sick, and Burial of the Dead; Processions; Floral Decorations; with Prayers before and after Service. Also, Brief Rules for Sacristans. With an Office for the Admission of a Chorister. 8d.; by post, 9d.

THE LITURGY OF THE CHURCH OF SARUM. Translated from the Latin, and with an Introduction and Explanatory Notes. By CHARLES WALKER, Author of "The Ritual Reason Why," "The Services of the Church according to the Use of Sarum," &c. With Introduction by Rev. T. T. CARTER, M.A., of Clewer; Dedicated by permission, to the late Bishop of Salisbury. 7s.; by post, 7s. 5d.

LITURGICAL, &c. (*continued.*)

PARAPHRASTICA EXPOSITIO ARTICULORUM CONFESSIONIS ANGLICANÆ. The Articles of the Anglican Church paraphrastically considered and explained. By FRANCISCUS A. SANCTA CLARA (Christopher Davenport). Reprinted from the Edition in Latin of 1646, with a Translation, together with Expositions and Comments in English from the Theological Problems and Propositions of the same writer, and with additional Notes and References. Edited by the Rev. FREDERICK GEORGE LEE, D.C.L. 7s.; by post, 7s. 5d.

RITUAL EXPLANATIONS. By Rev. C. J. ELIOT, sometime Fellow of Corpus Christi College, Cambridge. 4d.; by post, 5d.

The subjects dealt with are:—The Separation of the Sexes during Public Worship—The Rising of the Congregation at the Entrance and Departure of the Priests—Reverent Inclination of the Body at sundry portions of the Service—Choral Celebrations and Eucharistic Ritual and the Worship of non-Communicants—The mixing of a little Water with the Wine —The Sequence of Colours—Processions with Cross and Banners on solemn occasions.

THE BOOK OF COMMON PRAISE: HYMNS WITH TUNES FOR THE SERVICE OF THE CHURCH OF ENGLAND. Arranged and principally composed by C. E. WILLING, Organist of the Foundling, and late of All Saints', Margaret-street. To which are added Chants for the Magnificat and Nunc Dimittis, and Responses for Advent and Lent, as sung at All Saints; with fourteen new Double Chants, &c. 4s.; by Post, 4s. 3d. Also an Edition of the "THE TUNES" only. 2s.; by Post, 2s. 2d. An Edition of the "WORDS" only. 8d.; by post, 9d.

THE PSALTER, CANTICLES, AND THE PROPER PSALMS FOR CERTAIN DAYS. Pointed for Chanting by C E WILLING. 2s. 6d; by post, 2s. 9d.

ON RE-UNION, &c.

ESSAYS ON THE RE-UNION OF CHRISTENDOM. BY MEMBERS OF THE ENGLISH, ROMAN, AND GREEK CHURCHES. The Introductory Essay on Lutheranism, the Scandinavian Bodies, and the Church of the United States, is by the Rev. Dr. PUSEY. Contributors:—Rev. CANON HUMBLE; Sir CHARLES L. YOUNG, Bart.; Rev. C. A. FOWLER; Rev. G. NUGEE; Rev. PERCEVAL WARD; Rev. Dr. F. G LEE; the AUTHOR of the *Autobiography* in "The Church and the World;" H. N. OXENHAM, M.A.; A. L. M. PHILLIPPS DE LISLE, Esq.; DE Q.; the Rev. T. W. MOSSMAN; and a PRIEST of CONSTANTINOPLE. 6s.; by post, 6s. 4d.

SERMONS ON THE RE-UNION OF CHRISTENDOM. BY MEMBERS OF THE ENGLISH, ROMAN, AND GREEK CHURCHES. Contributors:—Revs. the Hon. C. L. Courtenay, H. N. Oxenham, T. W. Mossman, H. R. Bramley, J. M. Rodwell, Orby Shipley, C. Soanes, H. P. Liddon, J. Edwards, Jun.; Dr. Neale; Bishop of Cape Town; Dr. Fraser; Nicholas, Bishop of Antioch; J. M. Ashley; a Priest of the R. C. diocese of Westminster; T. T. Carter; Dr. F. G. Lee; T. W. Grieve; C. C. Grafton; W. J. E. Bennett; and Piasius, Bishop of Ephesus. First and Second Series. Each Volume 5s.; by post, 5s. 4d.

PHARISAIC PROSELYTISM: A FORGOTTEN CHAPTER IN EARLY CHURCH HISTORY. By Rev. R. F. LITTLEDALE, LL.D., D.C.L. 1s.; by post, 1s. 1d.

THE KISS OF PEACE; or, ENGLAND AND ROME AT ONE ON THE DOCTRINE OF THE HOLY EUCHARIST. By GERARD F. COBB, M.A., Fellow of Trinity College, Cambridge. Second Edition, enlarged to 680 pages. 7s. 6d.; by post, 8s.

SEQUEL TO THE KISS OF PEACE. 5s. 6d.; by post, 5s. 10d. (This new matter may be had separately by purchasers of the Original Essay.)

ON REUNION, &c. (*continued.*)

THE UNION REVIEW: A MAGAZINE OF CATHOLIC LITERATURE AND ART. By Contributors of the Anglican, Greek, and Roman Churches. In Bi-monthly Nos., 2s. each; by post, 2s. 2d. Annual Subscription, 12s. 9d., post free.

THE CATHOLIC EIRENICON, IN FRIENDLY RESPONSE TO DR. PUSEY. 6d.; by post, 7d.

A.P.U.C.—CORPORATE RE-UNION, NOT INDIVIDUAL SECESSION: Two Sermons at the 1868 Anniversary. By Rev. W. H. PERCEVAL WARD and Rev. Dr. LITTLEDALE. With the "Report" of the Progress of the Association from 1857 to 1868. 6d.; by post, 7d.

THE "SOUR GRAPES" OF DIS-UNION. A Sermon at All Saints', Lambeth. By Rev. F. G. LEE, D.C.L., on the 1869 Anniversary of the A.P.U.C. 6d.; by post, 7d.

A BRIEF COMPARISON OF THE FUNDAMENTAL DOCTRINES of the Anglican and Greek Churches. By the Rev. J. O. BAGDON, late English Chaplain in Zante. 1s.; by post, 1s. 1d.

THE FUTURE UNITY OF THE CHRISTIAN FAMILY. By the Rev. T. T. CARTER, Clewer. 1s.; by post, 1s. 1d.

A POPULAR ACCOUNT OF THE HOLY EASTERN CHURCH. Preface by Rev. Dr. LITTLEDALE. 3s. 6d.; by post, 3s. 10d.

PERE GRATRY'S FOUR LETTERS TO MONSIGNOR DECHAMPS, ON PAPAL INFALLIBILITY. 3s. 6d., cloth; by post, 3s. 10d.

THEOLOGICAL, DOCTRINAL, &c.

SERMONS, ON DOCTRINE AND PRACTICE. By the Rev. Dr. OLDKNOW, Bordesley, Birmingham. 4s.; by post 4s. 3d.

REDEMPTION: SOME ASPECTS OF THE WORK OF CHRIST CONSIDERED. By the Rev. R. M. BENSON, Evangelist Father, Cowley. 5s.; by post, 5s. 6d.

A DIGEST OF THE DOCTRINE OF S. THOMAS AQUINAS ON THE MYSTERY OF THE INCARNATION. By the Author of "A Digest of the Doctrine of S. Thomas on the Sacraments." 6s.; by post, 6s. 4d.

MEMORANDA OF ANGELICAL DOCTRINE FROM LADY DAY TO THE ASCENSION: being Notes on the Conception, Nativity, Circumcision, Baptism, Conversation, Temptation, Doctrine, Miracles, Passion, Death, Burial, Descent into Hell, Resurrection, Ascension, Session, and Judiciary Power of our Blessed Lord. By the Author of "A Digest of the Doctrine of S. Thomas on the Sacraments." 1s. 6d.; by post, 1s. 7d.

A DIGEST OF THE DOCTRINE OF S. THOMAS AQUINAS ON THE SACRAMENTS. By the Author of "A Digest of S. Thomas on the Incarnation." 4to. 7s.; by post, 7s. 5d.

THE BIBLE AND ITS INTERPRETERS: ITS MIRACLES AND PROPHECIES. By W. J. IRONS, D.D., Prebendary of S. Paul's and Rector of Wadingham, Lincolnshire. Second Edition. 6s.; by post, 6s. 6d.

THE SACRED WORDS OF OUR LORD JESUS CHRIST. (A Reading Book for Children.) By the Rev. Dr. Irons. 1s.; by post, 1s. 1d.

THE SACRED LIFE OF OUR LORD JESUS CHRIST. By the Rev. Dr. Irons. 2s; by post, 2s. 2d.

THE EVANGELIST LIBRARY CATECHISM. PART I. By the Evangelist Fathers, Cowley. 3s.; by post, 3s. 3d.

BY THE LATE REV. DR. NEALE.

SERMONS ON THE APOCALYPSE—On the Name of Jesus; and on the last Chapter of Proverbs. By the late Rev. Dr. NEALE. 5s.; by post, 5s. 4d.

SERMONS ON PASSAGES OF "THE PSALMS." By the late Rev. Dr. NEALE. 5s.; by post, 5s. 4d.

"THE SONG OF SONGS." A Volume of beautiful Sermons thereon. By the late Rev. J. M. NEALE. Edited by the Rev. J. HASKOLL. *Many are added which have never hitherto been published.* Second Edition, considerably Enlarged, 6s.; by post, 6s. 4d.

ORIGINAL SEQUENCES, HYMNS, AND OTHER ECCLESIASTICAL VERSES. By the late Rev. Dr. NEALE. 2s. 6d.; by post, 2s. 9d.

STABAT MATER SPECIOSA: FULL OF BEAUTY STOOD THE MOTHER. By the late Rev. J. M. NEALE. Now first translated. 1s.; by post, 1s. 2d.

HYMNS SUITABLE FOR INVALIDS, ORIGINAL or Translated, by the late Rev. J. M. NEALE. With a Preface by the Rev. Dr. LITTLEDALE. In paper cover, 6d.; by Post, 7d.; in cloth, 1s.; by Post 1s. 1d. A fine Edition on Toned Paper, cloth, 2s.; by post, 2s. 2d.

THE RHYTHM OF BERNARD OF MORLAIX, on the CELESTIAL COUNTRY. Edited and Translated by the late Rev. J. M. NEALE. New Edition, beautifully printed on Toned Paper. 2s. in cloth; by Post, 2s. 2d.; in French morocco, 4s. 6d.; by Post, 4s. 9d.; in morocco, 7s. 6d.; by post, 7s. 9d. Cheap edition 8d; by post, 9d.

HYMNS, CHIEFLY MEDIÆVAL, ON THE JOYS and GLORIES of PARADISE. By the late Rev. J. M. NEALE. Companion Volume to "The Rhythm of Bernard of Morlaix." 1s. 6d.; by post, 1s. 7d.

TEXT EMBLEMS: Twelve beautiful Designs, engraved by Dalziel, illustrating the Mystical Interpretation of as many Verses from the Old Testament. By the late Rev. J. M. NEALE. Second Edition. 2s.; by post, 2s. 2d.

BY THE LATE REV. DR. NEALE (continued.)

SERMONS ON BLESSED SACRAMENT. By the late Rev. J. M. NEALE, 2s.; by post, 2s. 2d.

NOTES, ECCLESIOLOGICAL & PICTURESQUE, on DALMATIA, CROATIA, &c.; with a visit to MONTENEGRO. By the late Rev. J. M. NEALE. 6s.; by post, 6s. 4d.

THE PRIMITIVE LITURGIES (in Greek) OF S. MARK, S. CLEMENT, S. JAMES, S. CHRYSOSTOM, AND S. BASIL. Edited by the late Dr. NEALE. Preface by Dr. LITTLEDALE. Second Edition. 6s.; by post, 6s. 4d. Calf, 10s. 6d. (for Presents); by post, 11s.

THE LITURGY OF S. MARK. And, **THE LITURGY OF S. JAMES.** In Greek. By the late Rev. J. M. NEALE. 1s. each; by post, 1s. 1d.

THE TRANSLATIONS OF THE PRIMITIVE LITURGIES OF SS. MARK, JAMES, CLEMENT, CHRYSOSTOM and BASIL, and THE CHURCH OF MALABAR. With Introduction and Appendices, by the late Rev. J. M. NEALE, D.D., and the Rev. R. F. LITTLEDALE, LL.D. Second Edition, enlarged. 4s.; by post, 4s. 4d.

THE HYMNS OF THE EASTERN CHURCH: Translated by late Rev. J. M. NEALE, D.D. New and larger type Edition. 2s. 6d.; by post, 2s. 9d.

"THE CHRISTIAN NURSE;" AND HER MISSION IN THE SICK ROOM. Translated from the French of Father Gautrelet, by one of the Sisters of S. Margaret's, East Grinstead; and Edited by the late Rev. J. M. NEALE. 2s.; by post, 2s. 1d.

A SERMON HELP—THE MORAL CONCORDANCES OF S. ANTONY OF PADUA. Translated, Verified, and Adapted to Modern Use, by Rev. J. M. NEALE; with Additions from the "*Promptuarium Morale Sacræ*" of THOMAS HIBERNICUS, an Irish Franciscan of the 14th Century. With Preface by Dr. LITTLEDALE. Second Edition. 3s.; by post, 3s. 2d.

ON MEDITATION, DEVOTION, &c.

CONFERENCES WITH GOD; being Meditations for Every Day of the Year. By C. C. STURM. Translated from the German by a Layman. Second Edition. 640 pages. 6s.; by post, 6s. 6d.

SHORT DEVOTIONS, primarily for the Young; with the Collects and Psalms of David. 1s. 6d.; by post, 1s. 8d. An Edition without the Psalms of David, 6d.; by post, 7d.

THE LITURGY OF THE CHURCH OF ENGLAND: An Altar Manual for Hearers or Communicants. Limp Cloth, 1s. 1d.; Stiff Cloth, 1s. 3d. Postage, 1d.

MANUAL OF DEVOTIONS FOR THE BLESSED SACRAMENT, ATTENDANCE, COMMUNION, PREPARATION, and THANKSGIVING. With Preface by the Rev. FREDERICK G. LEE, D.C.L. New 32mo. Edition, 1s.; by post, 1s. 1d. 12mo. Edition, 1s. 6d.; by post, 1s. 7d.

TRACTS BY THE EVANGELIST FATHERS, COWLEY. A packet of all Published. 1s. 8d; by post, 1s. 10d.

THE HOLY OBLATION; A Manual of Doctrine, Instructions, and Devotions relative to the Blessed Eucharist. By an ANGLO-CATHOLIC PRIEST. In roan, 2s.; in morocco, 4s.; postage 2d.

BISHOP WILSON (Sodor and Man) ON THE LORD'S SUPPER. Rubricated Edition. With Notes. In cloth, 2s.; in morocco, 5s. to 8s.; postage, 3d. A Cheap Edition (Rubricated), without the Notes, 1s.; by post, 1s. 1d.

BISHOP WILSON'S SACRA PRIVATA. Rubricated Edition. In cloth, 2s.; in morocco, 5s. to 8s.; postage, 3d.

THE SORROW OF JESUS. A Companion for Holy Week; intended for the use of Religious Societies. Third Edition. 1s.; by post, 1s. 1d.

ON MEDITATION, DEVOTION, &c. (*continued.*)

BUND'S AIDS TO A HOLY LIFE; in Forms of Self-Examination. New Edition, 1s.; by post, 1s. 1d.

PRAYERS AND NOTES: extracted from the MSS. of the late Sir Robert and Lady Wilmot, of Chaddesden: with Preface by the Rev. T. T. CARTER, Clewer. 7s. 6d.; by post, 8s.

SHORT PRAYERS FOR BUSY MEN AND WOMEN. From a Bodleian MS. 2d.; by post, 3d.

PRAYERS FOR CHILDREN; with **DEVOTIONS** for the HOLY SACRIFICE, HYMNS, &c. By Rev. F. G. LEE, D.C.L. With Frontispiece. 1s.; by post, 1s. 1d.

DEVOTIONS FOR SISTERS OF MERCY. Edited by the Rev. T. CARTER, Clewer. Part I.—For Daily Use, 1s. 6d.; by post, 1s. 7d. II.—Different Necessities, 1s.; by post, 1s. 1d. III.—Forgiveness of Sins, 1s.; by post, 1s. 1d. IV.—Holy Communion, 2s.; by post, 2s. 2d. V.—To the Holy Ghost, 1s.; by post, 1s. 1d. VI.—To our Lord, 1s.; by post, 1s. 1d. VII.—On The Passion, 1s.; by post, 1s. 1d. VIII.—On Sickness, 1s. 6d.; by post, 1s. 7d. Two vols., cloth, 10s.; postage, 8d.

THE LITTLE HOURS FOR BUSY PERSONS. By an ASSOCIATE of the CLEWER SISTERHOOD. 4d.; by post, 4½d.

SIX STEPS TO PERFECTION. Cut from the Works of M. Olier. By same Author. 4d.; by post, 4½d.

HINTS ON RELIGIOUS EDUCATION. By same Author. 6d.; by post, 6½d.

A PRAYER BOOK FOR THE YOUNG; or a Complete Guide to Public and Private Devotion. Edited by CHARLES WALKER. Second Edition, carefully Revised and Re-arranged. 700 pages. 4s.; by post, 4s. 3d. In various morocco bindings, 6s. 6d. to 12s. 6d.; postage, 6d. Cheap Edition, 3s.; by post. 3s. 2d.

THE LAST HOURS OF JESUS: being Colloquies on The Passion. From the German. 6d.; by post, 7d.

ON MEDITATION, DEVOTION, &c. (*continued.*)

REPENTANCE AND HOLY LIVING: being Meditations on the Lord's Prayer and the Seven Penitential Psalms. By the Rev. J. B. WILKINSON, Author of "The Parables," &c. 2s. 6d.; by post, 2s. 8d.

THE PARABLES OF OUR LORD: THIRTY-SIX INSTRUCTIONS THEREON; BEING PLAIN SERMONS ON THESE SUBJECTS By Rev. J. B. WILKINSON. 6s.; by post, 6s. 4d.

MEDITATIONS ON THE PENITENTIAL PSALMS. By the Rev. J. B. WILKINSON. 1s.; by post, 1s. 1d.

MEDITATIONS ON THE LORD'S PRAYER. By Rev. J. B. WILKINSON. 1s. 6d., by post, 1s. 7d.

SHORT DAILY READINGS AT FAMILY OR PRIVATE PRAYER, mainly drawn from Ancient Sources; following the Church's Course of Teaching for the Year. By Rev. J. B. WILKINSON. Vol. I., from Advent to Lent; II., Lent to Ascension; III., From Ascension to Sixteenth Sunday after Trinity. IV., completing Trinity-tide, with Readings for all the Saints' Days. In four Volumes. Separated, each 5s. 6d.; by post, 6s.

AIDS TO MENTAL PRAYER, &c. By Rev. J. B. WILKINSON, Author of "Daily Readings," "On the Parables," &c. 1s. 6d.; by post, 1s. 7d.

HOUSEHOLD PRAYERS. Preface by Dr. WILBERFORCE, Bishop of Winchester. 1s.; by post, 1s. 1d.

THE REFORMED MONASTERY; or, THE LOVE OF JESUS: A Sure and Short, Pleasant and Easy Way to Heaven; in Meditations, Directions, and Resolutions to Love and Obey Jesus unto Death. Preface by the Rev. F. G. LEE, D.C.L. (Being a Reprint of the said Work by Dr. BOILEAU, Chaplain to Dr. Fell, Bishop of Oxford, 1675.) 3s.; by post, 3s. 4d.

FENELON'S COUNSELS TO THOSE WHO ARE LIVING IN THE WORLD. Edited by W. J. E. BENNETT, Froome-Selwood. Large paper Edition, calf, 4s. 6d., by post, 4s. 8d. Cheaper Edition, 1s.; stiff cloth, red edges, 1s. 6d.; postage, 1d.

ON MEDITATION, DEVOTION, &c. (continued.)

FENELON ON FREQUENT COMMUNION. Edited by W. J. E. BENNETT, Froome-Selwood. 1s.; by post, 1s. 1d.

ADVICE TO THE YOUNG ON TEMPTATION IN SIN. By Monsignor DE SEGUR. 1s. 6d; by post, 1s. 8d.

PONDER AND PRAY: THE PENITENT'S PATHWAY. Translated by Rev. F. HUMPHREY. 2s.; by post, 2s. 2d.

THE DUTIES OF FATHERS AND MOTHERS. By ARVISENET. Edited by the Rev. G. C. WHITE, S. Barnabas', Pimlico. 1s. 6d.; by post, 1s. 7d.

AVRILLON'S DEVOTIONS AT THE BLESSED SACRAMENT. (Translated). 1s.; by post, 1s. 1d.

THE LITTLE WAY OF PARADISE. Translated from the Italian. 2s.; by post, 2s. 2d.

DEVOTIONS ON THE COMMUNION OF SAINTS. Compiled from the "Paradise for the Christian Soul," and other sources. For the use of English Churchmen. Part I.—Communion with the Faithful Departed. Part II.—Communion with the Saints and Angels. By CHARLES WALKER, Author of "The Liturgy of the Church of Sarum," "The Ritual Reason Why," &c. With Preface by RICHARD F. LITTLEDALE, LL.D., D.C.L. 2s. 6d.; by post, 2s. 8d.

THE RELIGIOUS LIFE PORTRAYED. Translated from the French. With Introduction by Rev. R. M. BENSON, Evangelist Father, Cowley. 1s.; by post, 1s. 1d.

ON CHRISTIAN CARE OF THE DYING AND THE DEAD. Illustrated. 3s. 6d.; by post, 3s. 9d.

THE OFFICE OF TENEBRÆ. (Published for the Guild of S. Alban.) 1s. 6d.; by post, 1s. 8d.

FASTING VERSUS EVENING COMMUNION. By F. H. D. 6d.; by post, 7d.

IMPRESSIONS OF THE AMMERGAU PASSION-PLAY. (1870.) By an Oxonian. 1s.; by post, 1s. 1d.

TALES, &c.

CHURCH STORIES FOR THE SUNDAYS, HOLY-DAYS, AND FAST-DAYS OF THE CHRISTIAN YEAR. In Fifteen Parts. Each, 1s.; by post, 1s. 1½d. Or, in Four Vols. Cloth, each 5s.; by post. 5s. 4½d.

CURIOSITIES OF OLDEN TIMES. A new work by the Rev. S. BARING-GOULD. 6s.; by post, 6s. 4d.

OSWALD, THE YOUNG ARTIST. A Tale for Boys. (Inculcating the necessity of a reverential attention when assisting in the Public Worship.) By C. WALKER, Author of "The Ritual Reason Why." 1s. 6d.; by post, 1s. 8d.

NORWEGIAN TALES; EVENINGS AT OAKWOOD. Translated by ELLEN WHITE. Preface by Rev. S. BARING-GOULD, Author of "Curious Myths," &c. 3s. 6d.; by post, 3s. 9d.

COUSIN EUSTACE; or, CONVERSATIONS WITH A DISSENTER ON THE PRAYER BOOK. By the Author of "Tales of Kirkbeck," "Aunt Atta," "Lives of the Fathers," &c. Edited by W. J. E. BENNETT. 5s. 6d.; by post, 6s.

RHINELAND AND ITS LEGENDS; with Other Tales. Translated from the German. By the Translator of "God still works Miracles," &c. With Preface by W. J. E. BENNETT. 3s. 6d.; by post, 3s. 9d.

GOD STILL WORKS MIRACLES. And Other Tales. Translated from the German of Töchter Album. By Author of "Rhineland and its Legends." 1s. 6d., in cloth; by post, 1s. 7d. Paper cover, 1s.; by post, 1s. 1d.

CHURCH BALLADS (First Series.) In a Packet of Twelve. 2s.; by post, 2s. 2d.

CHURCH BALLADS (Second Series) FOR THE FESTIVALS THROUGHOUT THE YEAR. Specially suitable for Young Persons or for use in the Parish or Schools. By the Author of "Church Ballads, First Series." 3s. 6d.; by post, 3s. 9d.

WAYLAND WELL: A Tale for Adults. By the Author of "Crystal Finlaison's Narrative," &c. 5s.; by post, 5s. 5d.

TALES, &c. (*continued.*)

ONLY A GHOST. By IRENÆUS THE DEACON. 1*s.*; by post, 1*s.* 1*d.*

LAME NED, THE CHORISTER. By CECILIA MACGREGOR. 1*s.*; by post, 1*s.* 1*d.*

DEEPDENE MINSTER; or, SHADOW AND SUNSHINE. By C. MACGREGOR. 1*s.* 6*d.*; by post, 1*s.* 7*d.*

SIR HENRY APPLETON: A Tale of the Great Rebellion. By the Rev. W. E. HEYGATE, Rector of Brighstone, Isle of Wight. 470 pp. 5*s.*; by post, 5*s.* 6*d.*

TALES OF KIRKBECK. First and Second Series. By Author of "Cousin Eustace," &c. Preface by W. J. E. BENNETT. Each Vol. 3*s.* 6*d.*; by post, 3*s.* 10*d.*

"OUR DOCTOR'S NOTE-BOOK;" Third Series of "Tales of Kirkbeck." 2*s.* 6*d.*; by post, 2*s.* 8*d.*

A COMMONPLACE STORY: by Author of "Cousin Eustace," "Tales of Kirkbeck," &c. Edited by W. J. E. BENNETT. 3*s.* 6*d.*; by post, 3*s.* 10*d.*

LIVES OF THE FATHERS OF THE CHURCH IN THE FOURTH CENTURY. By the Author of "Tales of Kirkbeck," "Aunt Atta," &c. Edited by W. J. E. BENNETT. In two Volumes. Each 5*s.*; by post, 5*s.* 4*d.*

AUNT ATTA. A Tale for Little Nephews and Nieces. By Author of "Tales of Kirkbeck," &c. Edited by W. J. E. BENNETT. 3*s.* 6*d.*; by post, 3*s.* 10*d.*

AUNT ATTA AGAIN; or, THE LONG VACATION. Edited by W. J. E. BENNETT. 3*s.* 6*d.*; by post, 3*s.* 10*d.*

THE FARM OF APTONGA: A Story of the Times of S. Cyprian. By the late Dr. NEALE. 2*s.*; by post, 2*s.* 2*d.*

OUR CHILDHOOD'S PATTERN: BEING NINE TALES BASED ON INCIDENTS IN THE LIFE OF THE HOLY CHILD JESUS. 2*s.* 6*d.*; by post, 2*s.* 9*d.*

THE CHILDREN'S GUILD. By Author of "The Abbey Farm." 2*s.* 6*d.*; by post, 2*s.* 9*d.*

TALES, &c. (*continued.*)

DAYS AT LEIGHSCOMBE. A New Tale for Children. 2s.; by post, 2s. 2d.

A LONG DAY. By the Author of "Days at Leighscombe." 6d.; by post, 7d.

USE OF A FLOWER. By the Author of "Days at Leighscombe." 9d.; by post, 9½d.

FROM DARKNESS TO LIGHT. A new Confirmation Tale. 2s. 6d.; by post, 2s. 9d.

THE VICTORIES OF THE SAINTS: Stories for Children, from Church History. New Edition. By Rev. Dr. NEALE. 2s.; by post, 2s. 2d.

THE PILGRIM; AND OTHER ALLEGORIES. 1s. 6d.; by post, 1s. 8d.

HENRY OF EICHENFELS, AND CHRISTMAS EVE. Two Stories from the German. By Rev. W. B. FLOWER. 1s.; by post, 1s. 1d.

REGINALD GRÆME; By the Rev. CLAUDE MAGNAY. 1s. 6d.; by post, 1s. 8d.

BLANCHE MORTIMER. By E. M. S. 2s.; by post, 2s. 2d.

THE LIFE OF S. PAUL. By Rev. Dr. BIBER. 2s.; by post, 2s. 3d.

HISTORICAL LECTURES ON THE EARLY BRITISH, ANGLO-SAXON, AND NORMAN PERIOD. Intended for the Use of Teachers of English History. By Mrs. FRANCES A. TREVELYAN. Partly Edited by the late Rev. CHARLES MARRIOTT, Oriel College, Oxford. (I. Roman Invasion to the Norman Conquest. II. William I. to Henry II. III. Henry II. to Henry III.) Each Volume 7s. 6d.; by post, 8s.

A SEQUENCE OF SYMBOLS FOR THE CHURCH SEASONS AND FESTIVALS OF THE CHURCH. Nine exquisite Illuminations. 21s.; postage, 8d.

SPANISH TOWNS AND SPANISH PICTURES. By Mrs. W. A. TOLLEMACHE. With many Photographs, Maps, &c. 7s. 6d.; by post, 8s.

J. T. HAYES, LYALL PLACE, EATON SQUARE;
AND
4, HENRIETTA STREET, COVENT GARDEN.

www.ingramcontent.com/pod-product-compliance
Lightning Source LLC
Chambersburg PA
CBHW030428300426
44112CB00009B/910